The Unofficial
BRIDGERTON
Cookbook

The Unofficial BRIDGERTON Cookbook

From The Viscount's Mushroom Miniatures *and*
The Royal Wedding Oysters *to* Debutante Punch
and The Duke's Favorite Gooseberry Pie,
100 Dazzling Recipes Inspired by Bridgerton

LEX TAYLOR

Adams Media
New York London Toronto Sydney New Delhi

Adams Media
An Imprint of Simon & Schuster, Inc.
100 Technology Center Drive
Stoughton, Massachusetts 02072

First Adams Media hardcover edition November 2021

ADAMS MEDIA and colophon are trademarks of Simon & Schuster.

For information about special discounts for bulk purchases, please contact Simon & Schuster Special Sales at 1-866-506-1949 or business@simonandschuster.com.

The Simon & Schuster Speakers Bureau can bring authors to your live event. For more information or to book an event contact the Simon & Schuster Speakers Bureau at 1-866-248-3049 or visit our website at www.simonspeakers.com.

Interior design by Colleen Cunningham
Interior photographs by Harper Point Photography
Chefs: Chase Elder, Christine Tarango, Martine English
Interior illustrations © 123RF/alexzaitsev, Sergey Kokesov; Getty Images/Snusmumr, the8monkey, TheModernCanvas, Infografx

Manufactured in the United States of America

10 9 8 7 6 5 4 3 2 1

Library of Congress Cataloging-in-Publication Data
Names: Taylor, Lex, author.
Title: The unofficial Bridgerton cookbook / Lex Taylor.
Description: First Adams Media hardcover edition. | Stoughton, MA: Adams Media, 2021. | Includes index.
Identifiers: LCCN 2021032946 | ISBN 9781507216729 (hc) | ISBN 9781507216712 (ebook)
Subjects: LCSH: Cooking, English. | Cooking, European. | LCGFT: Cookbooks.
Classification: LCC TX717 .T379 2021 | DDC 641.5942--dc23
LC record available at https://lccn.loc.gov/2021032946

ISBN 978-1-5072-1672-9
ISBN 978-1-5072-1671-2 (ebook)

Always follow safety and commonsense cooking protocols while using kitchen utensils, operating ovens and stoves, and handling uncooked food. If children are assisting in the preparation of any recipe, they should always be supervised by an adult.

For Mateo and Zoe.

Contents

CHAPTER 2

LUNCHEON DELIGHTS • 43

CHAPTER 3

AFTERNOON TEA • 71

CHAPTER 4

THE GRAND BANQUET • 107

Soups • 109

Vegetables and Leafy Greens • 123

Fish • 145

Meats • 163

CHAPTER 5

EVENING SWEETS AND LIBATIONS • 185

Acknowledgments

Like all things *Bridgerton*, the writing of this book was quite the family affair—though dreadfully lacking in scandal, I must say! First and foremost, I'd like to thank my sister, Marina, for her incomparable contributions. It is not uncommon in our family for even the lords and ladies to roll up their sleeves from time to time and prepare something for the evening feast, and Marina worked as hard as a scullery maid to prepare many of the toothsome delicacies found in the coming chapters. I'd also like to thank my parents, the Viscountess Diana and Viscount Eric, whose boundless help with recipes and editing made this book possible. I'd also like to give a big thanks to the talented mixologist, @misslizfurlong, for all her extraordinary help. Lastly, I want to thank my agent, Adam, for always having faith in me and for making this amazing project happen.

Introduction

Welcome to *Bridgerton*! It's springtime, and Grosvenor Square is abuzz with an electrifying air of excitement—not just because the social season has begun, bringing a silken tempest to every courtyard and banquet hall, but also because of all the scandal and stories that blow in with it. All eyes are on the first ball of the social season. Soaring music, glistening lights, and lavish decors all set the stage for a spectacle of pageantry and pomposity.

The Bridgerton and Featherington ladies arrive, adorned in pastel silk gowns and jewels, and the handsome lords don dress coats with their long square tails and ruffled lace (and some serious sideburns!). While watching *Bridgerton*, you are witness to the opulent lifestyles of the Regency era on vivid display. And of course, this includes the food. The Regency era (1811–1820) was marked by an infatuation with the exotic. In the new British Empire (after Napoléon's defeat at the battle of Waterloo in 1815), rare spices from the British colonies have become all the rage, and celebrity chefs whip these up into dizzying displays of edible architecture. Romance is food and food is romance, and like the waltz, the two go hand in hand. And, just like watching Daphne and Simon burn for each other, cooking, too, is a balance of passion and restraint.

The Unofficial Bridgerton Cookbook is your personal invitation into this time of glamour and gowns, courier notes, and nuanced gestures of desire. Whether you are trying to entice a handsome Duke of Hastings with gooseberry pie, or offering breakfast biscuits to a desperate Lord Berbrooke, this menu is fit for Queen Charlotte. With one hundred dishes (some virtuous and some scandalous) based on the characters and time period you love, *The Unofficial Bridgerton Cookbook* is a new and exciting way to engage with the show: First we had fan fiction, then fan art, and now fan food!

Experience *Bridgerton* like never before with mouthwatering recipes from a time known for lavish spreads of fresh fish and vegetables; roasted meats; pickles; and of course, hot and savory buns, tarts, and pies. But, like the show, this book does away with stuffy conventions and stirs up modern and multicultural twists that will leave you breathless. Whether you're serving your own duke, or trying to impress your queen, *The Unofficial Bridgerton Cookbook* explores foods and drinks featured in *Bridgerton*, like Regency Pie and Winning Pig Bacon Bites, along with favorites of the era such as Dainty Miniatures with Pickled Vegetables and savory Royal Indulgence Biscuits with Gravy. Slip into something elegant, dear reader: We're headed to the ball!

CHAPTER 1

A Royal Start to the Day

Just because it's breakfast doesn't mean it's not time for theatrics. For a family of means such as the Bridgertons, living in a time of lavish wealth and with a kitchen staff the size of a proper restaurant, breakfast is an opportunity to apply a little flair to the humble biscuit! Even the most fashionable members of London society adore this breakfast treat. It's time to polish the family sterling and draw back the curtains in the breakfast room.

One never knows when a possible suitor or guest with means and influence may come calling, and it would be pertinent to have a proper display of the morning's breakfast fares and settings. Biscuits, pies, fruit tarts, buns, jams, kippers, eggs, and of course bacon must all be displayed on a long table, preferably in the morning light and accented with roses, lilacs, and floral-themed pastries if one is feeling particularly ostentatious. The Bridgertons would be sure to showcase their family colors of modest hues of blue, green, and pink, whereas the Featheringtons would go with brighter hues of yellow and orange—whether this choice is a conscious one by the Baroness Featherington and Lord Featherington to hide their ignominious morality is merely speculation, of course.

The Beau Monde Biscuits

A flaky, buttery biscuit is the proper way to start any day and give strength for all the flair and commotion that the social season demands. Biscuits of course can be eaten plain, but with creamy butter or some sweet jam, they beckon the heavens indeed. And for nourishment before a fox hunt, serve the lords biscuits with hot gravy and bacon.

MAKES 6 BISCUITS

2 cups all-purpose flour
¾ teaspoon kosher salt
1 tablespoon baking powder
½ cup cold unsalted butter, cut into small cubes
1 cup buttermilk

1. Preheat oven to 400°F. Grease a baking sheet with nonstick cooking spray.

2. In a large bowl, combine flour, salt, and baking powder. Add butter to flour mixture. Mix, rubbing butter pieces with your fingers to break up and incorporate into mixture. Or add mixture to a food processor and pulse a few times.

3. Slowly mix in buttermilk with a spoon, using minimal mixing to get contents generally wet. Dip your hands in water and then quickly stir mixture with your hands to feel out any dry pockets and fold them.

4. Rewet your hands, and separate dough into six equal parts. Form into discs about 1" thick and lay out on prepared baking sheet with space between each disc.

5. Bake 20–25 minutes until biscuits turn golden. Let cool 5 minutes before serving.

....

THE BEAU MONDE

The beau monde, the fashionable world of high society, displayed its discerning tastes at every turn. Whether guests glanced toward the food, the flowers, or the majestic pineapple at the center of the table, they knew at once whether their hostess had achieved the dernier cri. Pity those who fell short!

Francesca's Fried Dough

As Francesca's older siblings are of age and in the marriage market, hopeful suitors come tapping on the Bridgerton door like rain on a roof. Watching the gift-bearing gentlemen in suits of all colors is truly a theatrical sight to behold—and a constant source of entertainment for the rest of the family. Fried dough balls are perfect for the occasion. They boast a magnificent crunch and a warm, soft center to sink one's teeth into. Serve with confectioners' sugar, whipped cream and berries, or roasted meats with cheese and pickles.

MAKES 8 BUNS

2$\frac{1}{2}$ cups all-purpose flour
4 teaspoons light brown sugar
2 teaspoons baking powder
$\frac{3}{4}$ teaspoon salt
1$\frac{1}{2}$ cups buttermilk (or 1$\frac{1}{2}$ cups whole milk with 1 tablespoon apple cider vinegar)
Canola oil, for frying

1. Preheat deep fryer with enough oil to cover dough balls to 375°F. Line a large plate with paper towels.

2. In a medium bowl, combine dry ingredients. Slowly add buttermilk while stirring until dough is wet and sticky.

3. Lightly flour your hands and form dough into eight balls. Carefully add balls to deep fryer, avoiding crowding. Add in batches depending on size of fryer. Fry until golden brown, about 5 minutes.

4. Remove buns from fryer with a slotted spoon or tongs and set on prepared plate to remove excess oil before serving.

BROWN SUGAR

Brown sugar, like all sugar coming from the British colonies, was valuable in the 1800s (though less expensive than granulated sugar). During the Regency era, the consumption of sugar became widespread. Everybody, not just members of the ton, wanted sugar in their tea, in their coffee, in their chocolate, and in other delicacies. Ample supplies made it possible for a luxury item such as sugar to become democratized.

Daphne's Maiden Oats

Much like the rays of the morning sun brighten the soul and lift the spirits, this porridge is a shining sight for sore eyes. It's wholesome, and it tastes simply divine. It is also well known that oatmeal cures many maladies of the heart, making it perfect for the ups and downs of the social season. Enjoy in the drawing room as Daphne practices the pianoforte.

SERVES 2

1 cup steel-cut oats
4 cups water
$\frac{1}{16}$ teaspoon salt
$\frac{1}{2}$ cup golden raisins
$\frac{1}{2}$ teaspoon ground cinnamon
2 tablespoons amber honey

1. In a small pot over low heat, add oats, water, and salt and stir often until thickened, 10–15 minutes.
2. Add raisins, cinnamon, and honey and continue to cook 2–3 minutes until raisins are soft. Serve in two medium bowls.

HONEY

Honey is delicious and savory, with a spectrum of colors and flavors depending on the nectars from the flowers involved, but think also about the bee! It makes twenty-five round trips a day, circulating within a mile of its hive to bring back a fraction of its weight in nectar. The Bridgertons' beekeeper's or gardener's work includes harvesting the honey, heating it, and filtering the syrup to create a virtual phantasmagoria of flavors and colors to add delicacy, taste, consistency, and sweetness to cooking or baking.

Bejeweled Oatmeal

A most modest and virtuous breakfast, this recipe features oats that are often brushed aside for the more alluring prospects of faster-cooking varieties. But the slow-cooking steel-cut oats are indeed the true gems of this dish. With their sensual textures and ability to complement fresh and dried fruits, nuts, and spices, they make a healthy, wholesome, and honorable way to breakfast. Heaven knows when we'll need that extra bit of energy!

SERVES 4

For Oatmeal
1 cup steel-cut oats
4 cups water
$\frac{1}{16}$ teaspoon salt
2 tablespoons heavy cream
$\frac{1}{2}$ teaspoon ground cinnamon

For Fruit Compote
2 medium Honeycrisp apples, cored and sliced (peeling optional)
$\frac{1}{2}$ pint fresh berries of choice
1 tablespoon amber honey
2 cinnamon sticks
$\frac{1}{3}$ cup raisins
$\frac{1}{2}$ teaspoon lemon zest
1 tablespoon rum or bourbon
2 tablespoons water or fruit juice

1. To make Oatmeal: In a small saucepan over low heat, add oats, water, and salt. Stir often until thickened, about 30 minutes.

2. Add cream and cinnamon and continue stirring until thick. Remove from heat.

3. To make Fruit Compote: Preheat oven to 375°F.

4. Place apples, berries, honey, cinnamon sticks, raisins, lemon zest, and rum or bourbon in a medium greased baking dish. Mix lightly. Mix in water or fruit juice.

5. Bake uncovered 40 minutes or until apples are soft. Spoon over Oatmeal in serving bowls. (Compote will last 5 days in the refrigerator.)

. . . .

STEEL-CUT OATS

Gruel was a common dish in the 1800s, consisting of oatmeal, butter, and some wine. People would also eat this dish in the evening hours for warmth. Today's steel-cut oats are derived from whole grain, or groats, cut up to shorten cooking time.

Household Hasty-Bake
Oatmeal Pies
with Sugared Berries

Whether one is taking an early trip to the country or simply prefers to take breakfast in the garden, these oatmeal pies are lovely on the go. They can be made with instant oats, and so are quickly made, in case one must flee an unwanted suitor or catch the vanishing sun! Garnish with Sugared Berries for a lavish look.

MAKES 4 (4") PIES OR 1 (9") PIE

For Sugared Berries
1/3 cup superfine sugar
1 large egg white, pasteurized
1 cup fresh berries of choice

For Oatmeal Pies
1 1/4 cups instant oats
1/2 cup all-purpose flour
1 stick unsalted butter
1/2 cup granulated sugar
3/4 teaspoon ground cinnamon
1/8 teaspoon salt
1/2 cup water
4 cups vanilla yogurt for filling
4 tablespoons amber honey

CONTINUED

1. To make Sugared Berries: Prepare a surface with wax paper. Place superfine sugar in a small shallow dish.

2. Whisk egg white lightly in a small bowl until bubbles form on the surface. Using a pastry brush, lightly coat each berry with egg white.

3. Gently roll berries in sugar and place on wax paper. Let dry 20 minutes.

4. To make Oatmeal Pies: Preheat oven to 400°F. Lightly coat four 4" pie pans (or one 9" pie pan) with butter and set aside.

5. In a food processor, pulse oats, flour, butter, sugar, cinnamon, and salt until butter pieces are no larger than a pea.

6. Pour mixture into a large bowl and mix in water until dough ball forms. If dough is too dry, add more water.

7. Separate dough into four equal parts and, using wet hands, press dough into pie pans. Make sure crust is even and without holes.

8. Bake 20 minutes until edges begin to brown.

9. Remove from oven and allow to cool 5 minutes. Fill with yogurt and Sugared Berries and drizzle with honey before serving.

MORNING HOURS

During the Regency, morning was generally considered to be any time before dinner, so it's not uncommon to hear of lunches and late snacks being taken in the "morning." Suitors dropped by in the "morning," say around five p.m., to pay respects, nibble on delectable berries or biscuits, and catch a glimpse of their beloved.

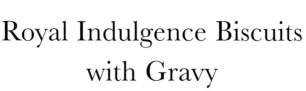

Royal Indulgence Biscuits with Gravy

*Waiting to find true love may take more than one social season.
But while things cool off for the winter, warm up with hearty biscuits
and gravy. Watching these two dance upon the plate is enough to
make even the most seasoned ton blush.*

MAKES 6 BISCUITS

3 tablespoons butter
1 cube beef bouillon
3 tablespoons all-purpose flour
2 cups whole milk
½ teaspoon kosher salt
1 teaspoon ground black pepper
1 batch The Beau Monde Biscuits (see recipe in this chapter)

1. In a small saucepan over medium-low heat, melt butter. Crumble bouillon cube into powder and add to pan. Slowly add flour until mixture forms a paste. Cook gently 2–3 minutes to remove flour taste.

2. Gently whisk in milk until gravy consistency forms. Add salt and pepper. Pour over Biscuits and serve.

BUTTERMILK

The buttermilk we use today has little in common with the one Regency-era cooks would have put in their biscuits. Back then, buttermilk was the watery and slightly sour liquid left over after churning butter. Today's cultured buttermilk is made out of sweet cream, adding a delicious flavor to these biscuits. Some things get better with time!

Daphne's Dearest Crepes

A favorite among French chefs for centuries, the simple crepe is coaxed into perfection with the most graceful and subtle of gestures—like the ever-so-delicate touch during a dance, an act both subtle and sensual. Just take note that crepes are seductive and may very well lead an unsavory suitor to come calling. Feel free to use your favorite fruits and top with additional butter.

SERVES 4

1½ cups all-purpose flour
1 tablespoon light brown sugar
¼ teaspoon kosher salt
3 large eggs
1½ cups whole milk
½ cup unsalted butter
1 tablespoon confectioners' sugar
1 cup fresh fruit (such as sliced bananas, blueberries, and sliced strawberries)

1. In a large bowl, mix flour, brown sugar, and salt. Add eggs and milk and whisk thoroughly.

2. Add 1 tablespoon butter to an 8" nonstick pan over medium heat. Once butter is melted and browning, add 5 tablespoons batter and swirl pan around so batter forms a thin circle. Cook 1–2 minutes per side until edges begin to crisp.

3. Transfer crepe to a large plate and repeat with remaining batter, adding 1 tablespoon butter to pan between every crepe.

4. Dust crepes with confectioners' sugar and serve with fresh fruit.

. . . .

CREPES

The name *crepe* comes from *crispus*, the Latin word for "curled" or "wrinkled." It is believed that crepes came about by accident—some batter spilled on a hot pan. However they started, they've been around for a long time, and variations continue to appear all over the world. They are *that* delicious.

Boxer's Best Sausage Doughnuts

There are days when even dapper dukes would prefer to lounge around in their undergarments and read the latest Whistledown paper than attend to the day's affairs, particularly after a rowdy night of placing bets and drinking at the ring. These doughnuts combine spices and flavors to make a morning treat you'll crave no matter how exhausted you are.

MAKES 10 DOUGHNUTS

1 pound ground pork
$\frac{1}{4}$ teaspoon ground cardamom
$\frac{1}{8}$ teaspoon ground nutmeg
1 teaspoon kosher salt
1 teaspoon ground black pepper
$\frac{1}{3}$ cup all-purpose flour
1 cup whole milk
2 large eggs, beaten
$\frac{1}{2}$ cup panko bread crumbs
Canola or peanut oil, for frying

1. In a large saucepan over medium-high heat, add pork, cardamom, nutmeg, salt, and pepper. Cook 10 minutes or until pork reaches an internal temperature of at least 145°F. Once cooked thoroughly, add flour and stir. Add milk and stir.

2. Continue to cook while stirring constantly 3 minutes, then remove from heat. Cover and refrigerate 2 hours up to 1 day.

3. Take about ⅓ cup sausage and roll out so it is 6"–8" long. Form it into a circle, connecting the ends. Repeat with remaining sausage to form ten "doughnuts."

4. In a deep fryer or in a large pot, heat enough oil to cover doughnuts to 375°F.

5. Place egg in a small shallow bowl. Place bread crumbs in a medium shallow bowl. Dip each doughnut in egg, then bread crumbs. Fry each doughnut 5 minutes or until golden brown. Allow to cool 5 minutes before serving.

. . . .

DOUGHNUT

Though there is a lot of controversy about who invented the doughnut, the earliest recipe, called "dow nuts," was invented in England around 1800 and involved frying a mixture of flour, sugar, eggs, nutmeg, yeast, and possibly butter in pig fat.

High Society Scones

All eyes are on these steaming and soft scones, a staple of any proper breakfast arrangement. One must add only a touch (or a lot) of butter or marmalade to experience complete breakfast bliss. Feel free to add spices or fresh herbs. There is very little you can't do with a scone. Store in the cold room (refrigerator) and serve with meats for a quick supper or snack. If you don't have barberries, currants or cranberries work well.

MAKES 12 SCONES

$\frac{1}{2}$ **cup barberries**

$\frac{1}{16}$ **teaspoon ground saffron**

2 cups all-purpose flour

4 teaspoons baking powder

1 teaspoon salt

2 tablespoons granulated sugar, divided

5 tablespoons very cold unsalted butter, cut into small chunks

3 large eggs, divided

$\frac{3}{4}$ **cup whole milk**

1 teaspoon water

1. Preheat oven to 450°F and set out two lined baking sheets.

2. In a small bowl, soak barberries in warm water for 30 minutes. In a separate small bowl, crumble saffron into 1 tablespoon water and set aside.

3. Add flour, baking powder, salt, 1 tablespoon sugar, and butter to a food processor and pulse until a very fine sand forms.

4. In a medium bowl, beat 2 eggs, saffron water, and milk until well combined. Gently mix in contents of food processor until just combined. Drain and stir in barberries.

CONTINUED

5. On a clean, lightly floured surface, knead dough minimally and form into a rectangle 1" thick. Dough should be very sticky. Don't overwork. Use a 2" round cookie cutter or glass to cut twelve circles of dough, setting them on the baking sheet $2\frac{1}{2}$" apart.

6. In a small bowl, beat remaining egg and water and brush lightly onto scones, then sprinkle remaining 1 tablespoon sugar on top of scones. Bake 8–10 minutes until lightly browned.

7. Remove from oven and allow to cool 5 minutes before serving. Will last up to 1 week in refrigerator.

. . . .

BARBERRIES

Barberries are remarkable—not just because they are tasty in scones and jams, but because they also help relieve the bad tempers of the grouchiest among the ton. Good for heartburn, bile, colic, psoriasis, and diarrhea, these barberry scones help ease the pain of those who eat them, and even the grouch's relatives who don't.

Prudence's Breakfast Pudding

*Though traditionally thought of as a dessert, banana pudding makes
for an exciting breakfast to serve alongside biscuits or scones. Prudence takes
hers with granola and fresh fruits in the drawing room, while Philippa
belittles poor Penelope. We'll see who has the last laugh.*

SERVES 4

¼ cup granulated sugar
2 cups whole milk
¼ cup all-purpose flour
1 large ripe banana, peeled and cut into 1" slices
1 teaspoon vanilla extract
3 large eggs, beaten
¼ teaspoon kosher salt

1. In a medium saucepan over low heat, add sugar, milk, and flour and whisk constantly until mixture thickens, 4–5 minutes. Remove from heat and let cool slightly, about 5 minutes.

2. In a food processor on low speed, pulse banana and vanilla until smooth. Add milk mixture and pulse on low speed until mixed. Turn up speed to high and slowly pour eggs and salt into food processor. Mix until thick and combined.

3. Pour mixture back into pan to cook over low heat, about 2 minutes, stirring constantly.

4. Pour into a large bowl, cover, and let cool to room temperature, about 5 minutes. Refrigerate 1 hour before serving.

BANANAS

The Regency brought us not just the Bridgertons, but also the banana we know and love today: the Cavendish banana, named after the "Bachelor Duke," William Cavendish, the sixth Duke of Devonshire. Which lucky lady will become the Duchess of Devonshire? Did Lady Whistledown just speculate about the future Banana Duchess? Someone should control her pen!

The Soused Duke's Kippers

Alice Mondrich serves some very burnt and charred fish to cure Simon's headache after a night of drinking. Though not particularly appetizing when burnt to a crisp, kippers are quite the honored traditional breakfast, though they can be eaten at any time of day.

MAKES 8 KIPPERS ON CROSTINI

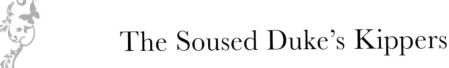

2 (4-ounce) fresh or canned herring fillets

¼ teaspoon sea salt

¼ teaspoon ground black pepper

3 tablespoons unsalted butter

1 (12") baguette cut into ½"-thick slices

4 tablespoons Clotted Cream (see recipe in Chapter 2) or cream cheese

¼ small red onion, peeled and finely diced

3 tablespoons chopped fresh parsley leaves

1. Preheat smoker to 300°F according to manufacturer's instructions. This can also be done in the oven at 300°F. Season herring with salt and pepper and cook 20 minutes on a large greased baking dish until herring reach an internal temperature of 145°F. Remove from heat and set aside.

2. Preheat oven to 400°F.

3. In a medium pan over medium heat, melt butter until it browns, 4 minutes. Remove from heat and set aside.

4. Place baguette on a greased baking sheet and bake 15 minutes until golden brown and crunchy. Remove from oven and let cool 5 minutes.

5. Spread Clotted Cream or cream cheese on crostini. Sprinkle onion onto crostini. Cut herring into eight 1-ounce pieces and place on top of Clotted Cream and onions. Top with butter and parsley, then serve.

HANGOVER REMEDIES

The saying "hair of the dog" (referring to alcoholic drinks believed to ease a hangover) was first used in England in the 1500s, and it referred to a real act where people who were bitten by a rabid dog would take hair from that dog and place it in their wound as a cure. And Simon seems to agree that the best way to cure a hangover provoked by an impossible love is to have another drink!

Penelope's Favorite Omelet

Why is this Penelope's favorite omelet? It could be because the delicate yellow color so perfectly resembles her dresses, or because the richness of the cream cheese and salmon really elevates the humble egg into a noble lord. Garnish with chives and, if you're feeling particularly cheeky, some hollandaise sauce (see recipe for Benedict's Perfected Cod à la Hollandaise in Chapter 4), which will further elevate the dish.

SERVES 1

1 tablespoon unsalted butter
2 large eggs
2 ounces sliced smoked (fully cooked) salmon
1 tablespoon cream cheese
$\frac{1}{8}$ teaspoon sea salt
$\frac{1}{8}$ teaspoon ground black pepper
$\frac{1}{2}$ teaspoon finely chopped chives

1. In a medium skillet over medium-low heat, melt butter. Using a rotating motion, turn pan to evenly coat with butter.

2. Whisk eggs in a medium bowl and add to pan. Gently rotate pan around to allow eggs to cover bottom.

3. Cover pan and cook over low heat 3 minutes until eggs are just barely cooked on the top.

4. Add salmon and cream cheese to eggs and fold in half. Cook 1 more minute. Season with salt and pepper.

5. Transfer to a large plate and garnish with chives.

SMOKED SALMON

Smoked salmon has been a delicacy among the ton ever since local markets started carrying Scottish salmon in the late seventeenth century. The sixteenth-century smokehouses in Scotland and later England smoked their fish in brick kilns or ovens. Smoking the salmon proved not only delicious, but also was a marvelous way to preserve fish before refrigeration. Yum.

CHAPTER 2

Luncheon Delights

For the glorious people of the ton, lunch is a show where everything matters. Whether attending a royal luncheon with the queen or hosting a lunch yourself, one must understand that first and foremost, this is a social event for the beau monde to dip their toes into the pool of improprieties and gossip. For even though the food served is elegant and provides nourishment for the body, gossip satisfies our endless taste for triumph and scandal. Only a royal spread of fresh fruits, meats, pies, and sandwiches, all on brilliant display, serves as a suitable backdrop to the whispers and secrets that are the true draw.

And what better than the recent gossip involving the scoundrel Lady Featherington and the desperate Marina for attempting to dupe poor young Colin? Seeing them kicked out of the luncheon was tastier than caviar! A word of caution, however: Much will be judged by the layout of your table, the sparkle of the family silver and china, the ornate ribbons, the lavish pies, and the colorful miniature sandwiches. Be sure to keep your guests gossiping about the food, not you!

Lady Cowper's Lobster Miniatures

Among Lady Cowper's many secrets, this recipe is perhaps her most unblemished. Lobster, the non plus ultra of lunch, is certainly a sign of true showmanship. As a small dish, this delectable combination of lobster and Saffron Aioli sits quite happily upon toasted white bread. If you're feeling creative, try serving it on a beignet cut in half. Or, if you fancy, why not offer this as the most decadent of hors d'oeuvres?

**MAKES 8 MINIATURES OR
16 OPEN-FACED SANDWICHES**

For Saffron Aioli
1 teaspoon saffron
3 tablespoons extra-virgin olive oil
1 cup mayonnaise
$1/4$ teaspoon salt

For Miniatures
2 tablespoons unsalted butter, softened
8 slices white or butter bread, crusts removed, cut diagonally
3 tablespoons Saffron Aioli (see recipe)
8 ounces cooked lobster meat
2 ounces chopped fresh mango
1 serrano or jalapeño, seeded and thinly sliced

1. To make Saffron Aioli: In a small pan over low heat, very gently heat saffron and oil for 3 minutes, then remove from heat and allow to cool in a small bowl.

2. Mix in remaining ingredients. Set aside.

3. To make Miniatures: Spread butter on bread and gently toast on medium heat in a medium skillet until golden brown, about 5 minutes. Or you can roll out each bread triangle before buttering and toasting for a crunchier cracker.

4. Spread 3 tablespoons Saffron Aioli on 8 bread triangles and top with lobster meat and mango. Garnish with thinly sliced serrano or jalapeño, then top with remaining toasted bread triangles. Remaining Aioli can be stored in a sealable container in the refrigerator for up to 1 week.

. . . .

SAFFRON

Saffron is worth more than its weight in gold. The chefs of the ton compete to create the finest concoctions with this luxury item. It takes seventy thousand crocus flowers and hundreds of hours of hands-on labor (making saffron the most expensive spice) to produce one pound of dried saffron. It has been used in cosmetics, in homeopathic treatments, and purportedly as a cleansing balm in a bath of mare's milk for queens.

Cucumber Miniatures with the Lady's Clotted Cream

Whether you're lunching with the queen or socializing over tea, miniature sandwiches are the perfect finger food, providing a convenient and elegant way to include a multitude of flavors to suit any palate. Here the freshness and crunch of the cucumber pairs divinely with the Clotted Cream for a simple yet elegant bite.

MAKES 8 MINIATURES OR 16 OPEN-FACED SANDWICHES

For Clotted Cream (Makes about 1½ cups)
1 pint heavy cream (not ultra-pasteurized)

For Miniatures
2 tablespoons unsalted butter, softened
8 slices white or butter bread, crusts removed, cut diagonally
4 tablespoons Clotted Cream (see recipe)
1 large seedless cucumber, peeled lengthwise into long ribbons
1 teaspoon salt
1 teaspoon ground black pepper
¼ cup fresh dill

1. To make Clotted Cream: Preheat oven to 170°F. Pour cream into an 8" ungreased baking dish and bake 8 hours uncovered until top becomes very light tan. Remove from oven and allow to cool to room temperature. Cover and refrigerate 8 hours or overnight.

CONTINUED

2. Pour out watery liquid, then flip remaining cream mixture upside down and, with a spoon, gently scrape bottom of skin to remove Clotted Cream. Discard harder top. Refrigerate Clotted Cream up to 1 week.

3. To make Miniatures: Spread butter on bread and gently toast in a medium skillet over medium heat until golden brown, about 5 minutes.

4. Spread Clotted Cream on 8 bread triangles. Fold cucumber ribbons and place on top of Clotted Cream. Add salt and pepper and top with remaining toasted bread triangles and garnish with dill.

. . . .

FINGER FOOD

Finger foods, or canapés, were extremely popular in the Regency era. Inspired by the French *canapé*, or "couch," the delicacies literally lie on top of the crispy toast or cracker beneath. There is more than one way to lie about during the hedonistic Regency era!

Philippa's Stilton Miniatures

It would appear, dear reader, that Mr. Finch and Philippa Featherington have found love in the most unlikely way: their love of cheeses. Philippa's Stilton Miniatures with Poached Pears are certain to bring you delight, and true love as well.

MAKES 8 MINIATURES OR 16 OPEN-FACED SANDWICHES

For Poached Pears
3 cups water
1½ cups granulated sugar
1 tablespoon amber honey
2 thin slices lemon
⅛ teaspoon ground cloves
1 teaspoon vanilla extract
2 medium Bosc pears, peeled and cored, quartered lengthwise

For Miniatures
2 tablespoons unsalted butter, softened
8 slices white or butter bread, crusts removed, cut diagonally
8 tablespoons Stilton cheese
Poached Pears and syrup (see recipe)

1. To make Poached Pears: In a medium saucepan over medium heat, combine all ingredients except pears and bring to a low boil. Once boiling, add pears. Cook pears at a very low boil 8–10 minutes if fruit is soft, or up to 25 minutes if fruit is hard, until transparent and fork-tender.

2. Remove pan from heat and allow pears to cool in poaching liquid 10 minutes. (After removing pears for Miniatures, reduce liquid over medium heat about 10 minutes to make a sauce.)

3. To make Miniatures: Spread butter on bread and gently toast in a medium skillet over medium heat until golden brown, about 5 minutes. Or you can roll out each bread triangle before buttering and toasting for a crunchier cracker.

4. Spread Stilton on 8 bread triangles, then cover with sliced pear and drizzle with sauce. Top with remaining toasted bread triangles.

STILTON CHEESE

Stilton cheese comes from England and can either include blue veins or not. It used to be served covered in mites and maggots that were eaten along with the cheese. It is known to cause strange dreams if consumed right before bed.

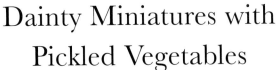

Dainty Miniatures with Pickled Vegetables

Some vegetables can be dreadfully boring, especially if they've taken a couple of days to arrive from the countryside. But this quick-pickling recipe works wonders in turning even dreary vegetables into sweet and refreshing teatime snacks colorful enough to liven up the linens. Or, serve alongside the night's game meat to help with digestion. This dish can be ready to serve in just a couple of hours in the event of unexpected guests. Note that the longer you pickle your vegetables, the more flavorful they become. But be careful! Let them sit too long, and they will become sour. Garnish with edible flowers to give your guests even more to talk about.

MAKES 8 MINIATURES OR 16 OPEN-FACED SANDWICHES

For Quick-Pickled Vegetables

1$^1/_2$ pounds assorted vegetables (such as seedless cucumbers,
carrots, red peppers), cut into $^1/_8$" slices

1$^1/_2$ cups superfine sugar (or granulated sugar blended in coffee grinder until superfine)

2 tablespoons kosher salt

4 medium cloves garlic, peeled and crushed

1 tablespoon ground white pepper

$^1/_4$ teaspoon ground coriander

$^1/_8$ teaspoon ground allspice

2$^1/_2$ cups apple cider vinegar

$^1/_2$ gallon cold water

For Miniatures

5 tablespoons unsalted butter, softened

8 slices white or butter bread, crusts removed, cut diagonally

Quick-Pickled Vegetables, cut into small pieces (see recipe)

CONTINUED

1. To make Quick-Pickled Vegetables: Add vegetables to a large sealable container. Add sugar, salt, garlic, white pepper, coriander, and allspice. Pour in vinegar until it comes to $\frac{1}{3}$ the height of vegetables. Pour in water, seal, and shake well.

2. Refrigerate at least 6 hours, up to 2 weeks.

3. To make Miniatures: Spread butter on bread and gently toast in a medium skillet over medium heat until golden brown, about 5 minutes. Or you can roll out each bread triangle before buttering for a crunchier cracker and then gently toast in a medium skillet over medium heat until golden brown, about 5 minutes.

4. Stack Pickled Vegetables on toasted bread triangles. Serve.

PICKLES

Unlike today, during the Regency era, vegetables were available only in summer. Pickling was done to preserve these vegetables for use in winter. It was also common to pickle eggs, meat, and fish in barrels. Pickles have been around for a long time—they were a favorite of Cleopatra's—and it is said that Napoléon paid an enormous reward in 1809 to the French chef Nicolas Appert, who found a way to pickle foods in glass containers, making it possible for Napoléon's troops to carry them for sustenance.

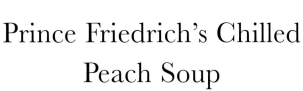

Prince Friedrich's Chilled Peach Soup

The fastest way to a lady's heart is through her stomach, and it would have been wise for Prince Friedrich to serve this to Daphne. This soup is charming and will surely make an indelible impression on the object of one's desires and attention. Serve on a hot day after a stroll through the gardens.

SERVES 4

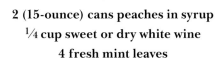

2 (15-ounce) cans peaches in syrup
¼ cup sweet or dry white wine
4 fresh mint leaves

1. Add peaches and syrup to a blender and blend until almost smooth. Add wine and blend until smooth. Cover and refrigerate 20 minutes.

2. Once chilled, divide into four medium bowls and garnish with mint leaves.

· · · · · · · ·

SOUP

Soups were very popular during the Regency era. Usually the first of the many foods offered at dinnertime, the soup bowls were placed on the table by the servants and taken off when guests had finished. The rest of the meats, fish, vegetables, sweet and savory pies, and other fine dishes remained on the table throughout the meal.

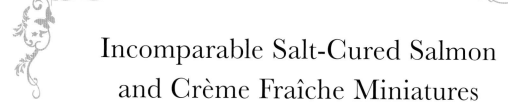

Incomparable Salt-Cured Salmon and Crème Fraîche Miniatures

If you are expecting the perfect suitor over for afternoon tea in the near future, then your first job is to have the kitchen staff prepare this dish. The salmon takes three days to cure, so this dish will not work for impulsive visitors. Those willing to wait will be enraptured by the creamy, decadent texture. Some claim it's better than smoked salmon, though you should judge this for yourself.

MAKES 8 MINIATURES OR 16 OPEN-FACED SANDWICHES

For Salmon

1 pound sushi-grade fatty salmon fillet

1 cup kosher salt

1 cup granulated sugar

1 teaspoon ground white pepper

1 small bunch fresh dill, stems removed, roughly chopped

For Mustard Dill Sauce

3 tablespoons Dijon mustard

2 tablespoons white balsamic vinegar

1 tablespoon granulated sugar

2 tablespoons finely chopped fresh dill

For Miniatures

5 tablespoons unsalted butter

8 slices white or butter bread, crusts removed, cut diagonally

4 tablespoons crème fraîche

Salmon (see recipe)

Mustard Dill Sauce (see recipe)

1 tablespoon salmon roe

2 tablespoons fresh dill

CONTINUED

1. To make Salmon: Gently rinse salmon under cold water, feeling for any bones that remain. Remove these with clean pliers. Pat dry and set aside.

2. In a medium bowl, mix together salt, sugar, and white pepper and pour into a 1-gallon sealable plastic bag.

3. Cover salmon with dill and place in a separate sealable bag. Seal bag and shake gently to coat salmon with mixture. Refrigerate 3 days, flipping once halfway through refrigerating.

4. Remove salmon from bag and rinse off under cold water to remove all mixture and dill. Lay salmon skin-side down. With a knife, remove any areas around edges that may have gotten hard or unsightly.

5. Starting at one end, make ⅛" slices. When making a slice, once the knife reaches the skin at the bottom, turn the blade sideways to remove fish from skin. Discard skin. Set slices aside.

6. To make Mustard Dill Sauce: In a small bowl, mix ingredients until sugar has dissolved. Refrigerate until ready to use.

7. To make Miniatures: Spread butter on bread and gently toast in a medium skillet over medium heat until golden brown, about 5 minutes. Or you can roll out each bread triangle before buttering for a crunchier cracker.

8. Spread crème fraîche on bread triangles, then top with Salmon. Drizzle on Mustard Dill Sauce. Garnish with salmon roe and dill and serve.

GRAVLAX

Gravlax originated in Sweden about five hundred years ago and was an early way of preserving salmon. Salmon would be buried in the sand along with spices, birch bark, and water and left to "cure." The result was as putrid as Lord Rutledge.

Gunter's Tea Shop Sipper

*Add a scandalous twist to the tea served at Gunter's Tea Shop
with this delightfully chilled recipe. Should you yearn for more sweetness,
you can try a sweeter liqueur or simply mix in a little brown sugar,
simple syrup, or honey in addition to the liqueur.*

SERVES 1

For Whiskey Infused with Black Tea
1 (750-ml) bottle rye whiskey
3 bags black tea

For Sipper
1 sugar cube
3 dashes Angostura bitters
2 whole roasted almonds, divided
**2 ounces Whiskey Infused with Black Tea
(see recipe)**
¼ ounce anise liqueur
1 dehydrated orange slice (optional)

1. To make Whiskey Infused with Black Tea: Place whiskey and tea bags in a large bowl and let soak 3 hours at room temperature. Remove tea bags and store covered at room temperature up to 3 months. (Makes about 25 ounces.)

2. To make Sipper: Add sugar cube to a mixing glass and drop bitters on cube to dissolve. Muddle cube if it doesn't dissolve on its own. Grate 1 almond into glass.

3. Add Whiskey Infused with Black Tea and anise liqueur to glass and fill with ice. Stir 20 seconds or until cocktail is very chilled.

4. Strain into a rocks glass with 1 large ice cube (or several small cubes). Grate remaining almond over cocktail. Garnish with orange if desired.

....

GUNTER'S TEA SHOP

Gunter's Tea Shop was an extremely popular pastry shop in
London that opened in the middle of the 1700s. The main draw was ice
creams and, later on, incredible wedding cakes made for royalty.

Promenade Pâté Miniatures

It's a sunny respite from the dreary and dull days of winter, and our beloved ton have taken to the park for a promenade. Lords wear their top hats in spectacular fashion, while the ladies don brilliant dresses and parasols. The air is fresh, and perhaps, if lucky enough, one may catch the slightest whiff of transgression. As it turns out, gawking can work up quite an appetite, so do bring along these delightful sandwiches to quell the hunger.

MAKES 8 MINIATURES OR 16 OPEN-FACED SANDWICHES

For Pâté
3 tablespoons unsalted butter
¼ cup minced shallot
1 medium clove garlic, peeled and minced
½ pound chicken livers
½ teaspoon fresh thyme leaves
1 teaspoon anchovy paste (optional)
1 ounce brandy
¼ teaspoon salt
¼ cup heavy cream
2 tablespoons capers

For Miniatures
2 tablespoons unsalted butter, softened
8 slices white or butter bread, crusts removed, cut diagonally
8 tablespoons Pâté (see recipe)
2 tablespoons fresh parsley leaves

1. To make Pâté: In a medium saucepan over medium-high heat, add butter, shallots, and garlic. Cook 3–5 minutes until shallots and garlic are browned. Add liver and thyme and cook, stirring often, 10 minutes until internal temperature reaches at least 145°F. Remove from heat.

2. Allow mixture to cool 20 minutes, then transfer to a food processor. Add anchovy paste (if desired), brandy, and salt. Pulse until smooth. Continue to pulse while slowly adding cream until mixed thoroughly. Add capers and pulse 2 seconds. Transfer mixture to a terrine and place in refrigerator to set 2 hours up to overnight.

3. To make Miniatures: Spread butter on bread and gently toast in a medium skillet over medium heat until golden brown, about 5 minutes. Or you can roll out each bread triangle before buttering and toasting for a crunchier cracker.

4. Spread Pâté on 8 bread triangles, then top with remaining toasted bread triangles. Garnish with parsley, and serve.

MEAT PIES AND PÂTÉS

Meat pies were beloved from medieval times. A favorite variation was the handheld pasty, made of ground beef, lamb, fowl, or fish and mixed with fat and spices. Larger amounts of filling were cooked in a terrine and covered with butter to prevent oxidation and spoilage. This mixture was what the French called *pâté*, and it reached its zenith with goose liver in 1775. Each area of the continent added its own variations to pâté.

Anthony's Approved Chicken Croquettes

Anthony is perhaps the most judgmental Bridgerton; since he's the oldest, he's had time to perfect this skill. These croquettes made to look like drumsticks are lovely for table adornment as well as pleasing the palate. They'll stand up to the most withering kind of judgment.

SERVES 6

For Chicken Dry Rub
1 tablespoon coarse sea salt
2 tablespoons chili powder
1 tablespoon ground white pepper
1 tablespoon garlic powder
1 tablespoon light brown sugar

For Croquettes
6 tablespoons Chicken Dry Rub
6 (4-ounce) chicken drumsticks
¼ cup all-purpose flour
¼ cup unsalted butter, softened
1 cup hot whole milk
1 large egg, beaten
1 cup panko bread crumbs
Canola oil, for frying

1. To make Chicken Dry Rub: Combine ingredients in a small bowl. Set aside.

2. To make Croquettes: Preheat oven to 400°F.

3. Apply Chicken Dry Rub to chicken, place in a large ungreased baking dish, and bake uncovered 45 minutes until internal temperature reaches 165°F.

CONTINUED

4. With a fork, remove meat from bones and set meat aside on a cutting board.

5. In a small pot, add chicken bones and enough water to cover the bones and boil over high heat until bones are clean, about 20 minutes. Pat bones dry and set aside to cool 10 minutes.

6. Chop chicken into small pieces and add to a medium pot with flour and butter. Cook over medium heat 3 minutes, then slowly stir in milk. Stir until thickened, about 2 minutes, and remove from heat and let cool, about 10 minutes.

7. Once cool, use your hands to make six balls with chicken mixture. Insert clean bones into each ball of chicken mixture and firmly form mixture around bone to resemble a drumstick.

8. Add egg to a small shallow dish and bread crumbs to a medium shallow dish. Add enough oil to a large deep pan to cover croquettes and place over medium-high heat. Heat to 375°F.

9. Roll "drumsticks" in egg then bread crumbs and fry until golden brown, about 4–5 minutes. Remove from oil and place on a paper towel to drain any excess oil and cool 5 minutes.

POULTRY

Chickens were not as popular to eat in the 1800s as they are today. They were generally prized for their eggs, which would have been a woman's duty to collect. Duck and geese were the preferred fowl for feasts, as they were larger and plumper than the smaller chickens of the Regency.

Simon's Quick-Dip Croquettes

Simon seems to use his napkin in a way that Daphne finds quite peculiar. It is only after she asks her maid, Rose, that she understands why he's a quick dipper. These scrumptious croquettes can be made in advance, up to one week, and fired up at a moment's notice.

MAKES 12 CROQUETTES

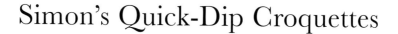

16 ounces cremini mushrooms, cut into ¼" cubes

1 medium shallot, peeled and diced

4 tablespoons unsalted butter

2 tablespoons all-purpose flour

1 cup whole milk

1 teaspoon ground black pepper

Canola or peanut oil, for frying

2 large eggs, beaten

2 cups panko bread crumbs

1. In a medium saucepan over low heat, add mushrooms and cook 10 minutes to remove water. Add shallots and butter and cook until shallots become tender, about 5 more minutes.

2. Whisk in flour, then add milk and stir until thick, about 1 minute. Add pepper, then remove pan from heat and let cool to room temperature, about 30 minutes. Once cool, transfer mixture to a medium sealable container and refrigerate 1 hour to set.

3. To a large, heavy-bottomed pot, add enough oil to cover croquettes. Heat to 375°F over high heat. Line a large plate with paper towels.

4. Place egg in a small shallow bowl. Place bread crumbs in a separate small shallow bowl. Separate mushroom mixture into twelve equal balls and roll into elongated ovals. Roll in egg, then coat in bread crumbs on all sides.

5. Fry until golden brown, 4–5 minutes. Place on prepared plate and pat dry to remove excess oil before serving.

. . . .

CROQUETTES

Croquettes were common on any Regency dinner table. They were considered "removes," or smaller plates that would be removed from the table once diners finished and replaced with another small dish. Larger and more grandiose dishes like large roasts and flummery would adorn the table the entire evening.

Benedict's Mushroom Miniatures

*A simple way to preserve mushrooms is by cooking out all the moisture
and then introducing some fats to hold them together. This creates a duxelles,
a thick, umami paste. A duxelles can also be used to cover the tenderloin
in a beef Wellington recipe for extra depth of character. Though Lord
Benedict hardly needs extra depth of character!*

MAKES 8 MINIATURES OR
16 OPEN-FACED SANDWICHES

For Duxelles
5 tablespoons unsalted butter, divided
1 large shallot, peeled and finely chopped
6 medium cloves garlic, peeled
1 pound cremini mushrooms cut into ⅛" cubes
1 teaspoon kosher salt
1 teaspoon ground black pepper

For Miniatures
2 tablespoons unsalted butter, softened
8 slices white or butter bread, crusts removed, cut diagonally
8 tablespoons Duxelles (see recipe)
¼ teaspoon sea salt
2 tablespoons fresh parsley leaves

1. To make Duxelles: In a medium pan over low heat, melt 2 tablespoons butter, then add shallots and garlic and cook until translucent, about 5 minutes.

2. Add mushrooms and cook 30–40 minutes, stirring often, until all moisture is evaporated. Add remaining 3 tablespoons butter, salt, and pepper and cook until butter is melted. Stir well.

3. Remove from heat and allow to cool to room temperature, about 30 minutes. Wrap mixture in plastic wrap and roll into a tube. Refrigerate until mixture is solid, about 2 hours. Remove from plastic wrap and cut into eight ½"-thick discs. Return immediately to refrigerator until ready to serve, up to 3 months.

4. To make Miniatures: Spread butter on bread and gently toast in a medium skillet over medium heat until golden brown, about 5 minutes. Or you can roll out each bread triangle before buttering and toasting for a crunchier cracker.

5. Place a slice of Duxelles on 8 bread triangles, sprinkle on some sea salt, then top with remaining toasted bread triangles. Garnish with parsley leaves.

MUSHROOMS

The word *mushroom* was often used during the Regency era as slang for someone obsessed with climbing the social ladder. Such a person had been known to sneak into parties and use flattery for personal gain.

Portia's Green Soup

To be tactless is one thing, but to bore your kind guests with an unflattering soup is a whole other matter. This soup is both glamorous enough to ignite attention (and envy), and light and invigorating enough to put that extra stride in your step for the evening's ball. Sadly for the Featherington daughters, it's often quite impossible to eat while trussed in their corsets. It's also a healthy dish. For an even more dazzling dish, top with your favorite garden delights: sliced radishes, chopped nuts, and salad greens make lovely garnishes.

SERVES 6

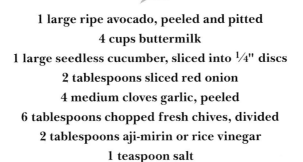

1 large ripe avocado, peeled and pitted

4 cups buttermilk

1 large seedless cucumber, sliced into $\frac{1}{4}$" discs

2 tablespoons sliced red onion

4 medium cloves garlic, peeled

6 tablespoons chopped fresh chives, divided

2 tablespoons aji-mirin or rice vinegar

1 teaspoon salt

Add all ingredients except 3 tablespoons chives to a blender and blend until smooth. Chill 1 hour. Serve in six small bowls garnished with remaining 3 tablespoons chives.

. . . .

AVOCADOS

Avocados came to Regency England on one of the two thousand ships that sailed into London every day. Originally from Mexico and Central America, their name comes from an Aztec word, *āhuacatl*, meaning "testicle." Their route went through Jamaica and the other British colonies. Back then, as now, people understood the avocado to be a fruit, not a vegetable, but the ton's chefs used them in special soups and vegetable mousse extravaganzas.

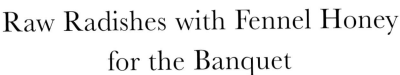

Raw Radishes with Fennel Honey for the Banquet

Absolutely perfect for a royal banquet or ball, a plate of these radishes on the banquet table commands respect and a bit of inspection. For who has ever seen such remarkable colorful bites? Serve these in the springtime when radishes are in season to brighten up the palate after heavier foods.

MAKES 12 RADISHES

12 large radishes, washed, stems removed
2 tablespoons amber honey
1 teaspoon fennel pollen or ground fennel
1 teaspoon sea salt

1. Add radishes to a large bowl and drizzle with honey.
2. Sprinkle with fennel and salt. Serve.

BALLS

Balls were at the center of Regency life for the ton. They were a place to see and be seen, to find love, and to eat! These fantastical events would each have their own theme and would revolve around formation dances that could last up to one hour each. It was customary that a woman must dance with any man who asked, unless she was engaged.

CHAPTER 3

Afternoon Tea

In *Bridgerton*, rumors spread as thick as double cream and are just as tasty. For those of leisure, being social is a great time to see and to be seen. And whether you're conversing with family in the drawing room or dallying about Grosvenor Square, taking tea in one of the shops, there are only two things on the mind: romance and, of course, food. Surely any principled host of the day would know that delicious treats can be as seductive and alluring as the most eligible prince. And if one stands a chance of acquiring a sought-after match, everything must be exquisite. The grand spread set forth for teatime is truly a symphony for the eyes and heart and, if executed properly, should eclipse the voracious urge for rumors and shame.

Dear reader, you may not be privy to the formalities of teatime, but for folks of fashion and leisure like the Bridgertons, teatime is an occasion for a sweet bite and a hot drink. Tea, like coffee, was expensive during the Regency era, and so teatime became a ceremony: another occasion to show off one's splendid sense of refinement and taste.

Scheming Ginger Tea–Glazed Honey Cake

Oh what a daring provocateur this cake is! With a tantalizing glaze, this cake is worthy of a full page of rapturous applause by Lady Whistledown. It would seem that few things in Bridgerton are as easy to heap praise upon as this honey cake. If you've been caught up in a scandal, it may be prudent to serve this gorgeous treat as a distraction.

SERVES 8

For Cake

2 large eggs

1 cup granulated sugar

$\frac{1}{2}$ cup canola (or other neutral) oil

1 cup amber honey

1 teaspoon vanilla extract

1 cup plus 1 tablespoon brewed ginger tea (strong; use a minimum of 2 tea bags and/or 2 tablespoons fresh grated ginger)

2 cups all-purpose flour

$\frac{1}{2}$ teaspoon baking soda

2 teaspoons baking powder

$\frac{1}{2}$ teaspoon ground cinnamon

$\frac{1}{2}$ teaspoon ground cloves

Zest from 1 small orange (optional)

For Glaze

$1\frac{1}{2}$ cups confectioners' sugar

3 tablespoons brewed ginger tea (strong)

1. To make Cake: Preheat oven to 350°F and grease a 6-cup loaf pan and three cups of a muffin tin with canola oil or another neutral oil.

2. In a stand mixer fitted with a paddle attachment, beat together eggs and sugar. Add oil, honey, vanilla, and 1 cup plus 1 tablespoon tea and beat thoroughly.

3. Add remaining ingredients and beat until just mixed, scraping down sides of bowl if necessary.

4. Pour batter into prepared pan and tin and bake 60 minutes or until a toothpick inserted in center comes out clean. Check muffins at 20 minutes for doneness, as they will bake faster than the loaf. (It's best to make Cake 2 days in advance to let flavors settle.)

5. To make Glaze: In a medium bowl, mix together sugar and 3 tablespoons tea until they form a thick paste. For a sheerer glaze, dilute cautiously with more tea.

6. Spoon Glaze over Cake. Bang cake pan and muffin tin gently a few times on the counter to help coax down some dainty drips. Allow glaze to set 10 minutes before serving.

. . . .

GINGER

Ginger cakes and ginger beer were enjoyed at all of the meals during the Regency period. The root of *ginger* means "antlers" in Sanskrit, and this ingredient was well known throughout Europe during the 1800s. Add sugar to ginger, and delicacies follow.

Mended Heart Sablé Biscuits

*These subtle, elegant cookies are real showstoppers. Like Daphne and Simon—
two individuals joined by love—this recipe features two separate doughs that make
a beautiful union when joined together. The cookies are firm, perfect for serving
with tea or coffee, and can be cut into any shape or sandwiched together
with a ganache filling. Enjoy with ratafia.*

MAKES 24 BISCUITS

1¼ cups all-purpose flour
⅓ cup almond flour
½ teaspoon salt, divided
¾ cup cocoa powder
⅓ cup plus 4 tablespoons granulated sugar, divided
½ cup unsalted butter, softened
½ cup confectioners' sugar
1 large egg
1 large egg yolk

1. Line two baking sheets with wax paper.

2. In a large bowl, sift together flours and ¼ teaspoon salt. In a medium bowl, mix cocoa, ⅓ cup granulated sugar, and remaining ¼ teaspoon salt. Set aside.

3. In a stand mixer fitted with a paddle attachment, beat butter and confectioners' sugar until well combined. Add egg and egg yolk and continue beating about 3 minutes until combined.

CONTINUED

4. Evenly divide butter mixture into bowls with flour and cocoa mixtures. Pour flour mixture back into stand mixer and beat until a firm dough forms. Set dough aside.

5. Pour cocoa mixture into stand mixer and beat until another firm dough forms. Knead each dough into a ball, cover with plastic wrap, and refrigerate 30 minutes.

6. Preheat oven to 350°F.

7. On a clean, lightly floured surface, knead chilled dough balls once or twice separately, then knead together until a marbling effect is achieved. Roll dough out to about ¼" thick, cut into heart shapes, and place on prepared sheets.

8. Sprinkle biscuits lightly with remaining 4 tablespoons granulated sugar and bake 12–14 minutes until firm and golden. Allow to cool on sheets 3 minutes, then transfer to a wire cooling rack to cool completely, about 20 minutes, before serving.

. . . .

RATAFIA

Ratafia can mean many different things but generally refers to a fortified wine or liquor flavored with almonds and spices. French ratafia is a wine with the addition of brandy. While this drink started in the Mediterranean, like many other delicacies, it found its way into London's high society.

Teatime Gooseberry Pie Lemonade

It would seem only appropriate, given its importance, that gooseberry pie is enjoyed in as many ways as possible, so this recipe reimagines the pie into a delightful teatime lemonade. And when the mood is light and the sun warms the drawing room, a refreshing tea is most acceptable.

SERVES 1

For Tart Lemonade
4 ounces fresh lemon juice
1 ounce simple syrup (equal parts granulated sugar and water blended until dissolved)
3 ounces water

For Gooseberry Pie Lemonade
20 grams (approximately 5) gooseberries or golden berries,
plus 1 sliced berry for garnish
1 teaspoon light brown sugar
3 sprigs fresh mint, divided
¼ teaspoon ground cinnamon
5 ounces Tart Lemonade (see recipe)
2 tablespoons confectioners' sugar

1. To make Tart Lemonade: Mix ingredients vigorously in a small bowl for 20 seconds.

2. To make Gooseberry Pie Lemonade: Add gooseberries, brown sugar, leaves of 1 mint sprig, and cinnamon to a cocktail shaker. Muddle ingredients slightly to release oils. Add Tart Lemonade.

3. Fill shaker with ice and shake vigorously 10 seconds. Strain into a julep cup or rocks glass filled with crushed ice. Garnish with remaining 2 mint sprigs, sliced gooseberry, and confectioners' sugar.

MEDICINAL BERRIES

During medieval times, gooseberries were used as medicine, as they were thought to reduce fever.

Purity Cookies

In the town houses around Grosvenor Square, one can quite literally taste the excitement for the upcoming season. Teatime is the perfect opportunity to serve up a display of all of one's accomplishments and great deeds in order to make good first impressions to boost one's chances for success. Almonds are a sign of virginity and purity, and thus are a most appropriate flavor for a potential suitor.

MAKES 10 COOKIES

¼ cup canola (or other neutral) oil
¼ cup amber honey
½ teaspoon almond extract
2 cups finely ground almond flour
½ teaspoon salt
½ teaspoon baking soda
¼ cup mini chocolate chips
¼ cup dry-roasted almond slivers

1. Preheat oven to 350°F. Line a baking sheet with parchment paper.
2. In a large bowl, combine oil, honey, and almond extract. Stir in remaining ingredients.
3. Roll dough into ten small balls and place on prepared baking sheet 2" apart. Bake 10–12 minutes until golden brown.
4. Allow to cool on baking sheet 10 minutes before serving.

TEATIME

The lady of the house presided over the tea table. This was her solo turn, her time to shine. The ceremony began when she was ready. The protocol was strict. Attendance was compulsory for family members and visitors.

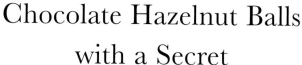

Chocolate Hazelnut Balls
with a Secret

Lord and Lady Granville have their own "arrangements" when it comes to their personal affairs. Far removed from the prying eyes of the ton, this colorful couple knows how to put on a show. For people can know only what they see. During their parties, they serve delicious date balls rolled in cocoa powder, hiding the sweet bliss within.

MAKES 10 BALLS

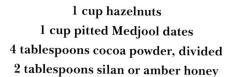

1 cup hazelnuts
1 cup pitted Medjool dates
4 tablespoons cocoa powder, divided
2 tablespoons silan or amber honey

1. Line a large rectangular sealable container with parchment paper.

2. In a food processor fitted with an S blade attachment, grind hazelnuts into a sandy mixture. Remove from processor and set aside in a small bowl.

3. Add dates to processor and grind until they form a sticky ball. Add hazelnuts back in, along with 2 tablespoons cocoa powder, and silan or honey, and mix until combined.

4. Roll into ten golf ball–sized balls. Roll each in remaining 2 tablespoons cocoa powder to cover. Place in lined container and refrigerate 20 minutes or until firm.

COCOA

In the Regency era, cacao beans were richly valued.
Queen Charlotte invited her most noteworthy guests to a
cup of hot cocoa or her favorite chocolate puffs!

Lady Featherington's Society Sponge Cake

Lady Featherington's lavish and colorful frocks seem outlandish, but perhaps they offer a necessary distraction from her misdeeds and transgressions. Regardless, when it's teatime and she has guests, she will most certainly serve a cake similar to this one, knowing that its grandeur will direct attention away from some of the unpleasantries about.

SERVES 10

For Macerated Berries
1 pound fresh berries, sliced (dry after washing)
¼ cup Moscato or other sweet wine
2 tablespoons granulated sugar or amber honey

For Sponge Cake
8 cold large eggs
1½ cups granulated sugar
⅓ cup canola (or other neutral) oil
⅓ cup pulp-free orange juice
2 cups all-purpose flour
2 teaspoons baking powder
1 cup fresh berries
1 teaspoon confectioners' sugar

1. To make Macerated Berries: Place all ingredients in a large bowl and stir gently. Cover and refrigerate 24 hours or until berries soften.

2. To make Sponge Cake: Preheat oven to 350°F. Line an 8" springform pan with parchment paper.

3. Using a hand mixer or stand mixer fitted with a whisk attachment, whisk eggs in a large bowl until stiff peaks form, about 10 minutes. Add sugar and whisk briefly.

CONTINUED

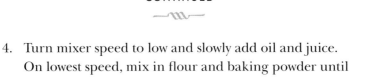

4. Turn mixer speed to low and slowly add oil and juice. On lowest speed, mix in flour and baking powder until just combined.

5. Pour batter into prepared pan and bake 60 minutes until a toothpick inserted in center comes out clean. Transfer immediately to a wire cooling rack, releasing from pan to cool upside down 1 hour.

6. Once cool, flip over so the rounded part is on top, and cut into 2 equal rounds. Spoon Macerated Berries evenly over one cake round, and top with second cake round. Top with fresh berries and dust with confectioners' sugar.

TON

The real-life ton of this era was different from preceding generations in that members commingled with Queen Charlotte, just as they do in *Bridgerton*. This shielded them from the laws of the regular folk and helped fuel their "anything goes" mentality.

Chocolate-Dipped Duke and Duchess Strawberries

Simon and Daphne know how to put on a spectacle. One simply must demonstrate what people want to see. And once all eyes are focused on you, give them a good show! These strawberries are used to being the center of attention and can shine bright enough for the whole ton to take heed.

SERVES 12

1 (10-ounce) bag milk or dark chocolate chips
1 pound fresh strawberries, hulled
$\frac{1}{2}$ cup white chocolate chips (optional)

1. Line a baking sheet with wax paper.

2. In a small microwave-safe bowl, heat milk or dark chocolate on medium in 30-second intervals, stirring well after each cook time until melted.

3. Holding a strawberry from the top, dip gently into melted chocolate, rotating for full coverage. Set on prepared sheet and repeat with remaining strawberries. Refrigerate 15 minutes.

4. Melt white chocolate (if using) in a separate small microwave-safe bowl on medium in 30-second intervals, stirring between cook times. Pour into a small sandwich bag. Snip a small hole in a corner of bag and drizzle white chocolate over chocolate-covered strawberries. Allow to cool completely, about 20 minutes, before serving.

WHITE CHOCOLATE

Alas, white chocolate was not known in the Regency era. A twentieth-century invention, it is made using cacao butter mixed with sugar and milk. It has a milder flavor than milk or dark chocolate. However, don't let this historical anachronism get in the way of decorating your gorgeous chocolate-covered strawberries!

Queen Charlotte's Puff Pomeranians

These precious little puffs are as sweet and revered as the queen's pups themselves. And though we cannot have the queen's Pomeranians, we can have as many of these treats as we would like. They are crispy and flaky and may end up in your lap.

MAKES 6 POMERANIANS

6 puff pastry shells

²⁄₃ cup mascarpone cheese

2¹⁄₂ tablespoons granulated sugar

¹⁄₈ teaspoon salt

1 (7-ounce) package marzipan

1 teaspoon chocolate frosting or chocolate ganache or edible markers

12 mini chocolate chips

1. Preheat oven to 425°F and line a baking sheet with parchment paper.

2. Separate and bake pastry shells on prepared baking sheet according to package instructions until golden and flaky. Set aside to cool completely, about 20 minutes.

3. In a medium bowl, whisk mascarpone vigorously 1 minute, then add sugar and salt and combine.

4. Remove and set aside the middle circle (lid) of each pastry shell. Pipe or spoon 2 tablespoons mascarpone mixture in each shell.

5. To decorate Pomeranian faces, mold marzipan into twelve triangular ears and six round or oval snouts. Press these to reserved shell lids using the mascarpone mixture as glue. Use a tiny dot of mascarpone to adhere chocolate chips as eyes.

6. Using frosting, ganache, or edible markers, pipe or draw a small brown nose and mouth onto marzipan snouts. Carefully stick a Pomeranian face onto each mascarpone-filled shell, then serve.

. . . .

MARZIPAN

Marzipan is one of the most delicious concoctions of human cuisine. A sweet paste made of almond and sugar, it has been enjoyed for centuries in the Middle East and the Mediterranean. Members of the ton used it to make Christmas and wedding cakes. Marzipan paste can also be sculpted into different shapes, painted with food dyes, and eaten with enormous pleasure!

Meringue Kisses in the Garden

Few things are as dangerous as an unwed couple being caught in the garden unchaperoned. All it takes is a single glance from an envious onlooker to shower shame and ruin upon the young couple. In this recipe, keep the egg whites and egg yolks separated, lest there be ruination.

MAKES 45 KISSES

2 large egg whites, at room temperature
$\frac{1}{4}$ teaspoon cream of tartar
1 cup plus 1 teaspoon superfine granulated sugar
$\frac{1}{2}$ teaspoon vanilla extract (optional)
Gel food coloring (optional)

1. Preheat oven to 200°F. Line two baking sheets with parchment paper.

2. In a stand mixer fitted with a whisk attachment, beat egg whites on medium speed until foamy, about 3 minutes. While mixer is still running, add cream of tartar and sugar 1 tablespoon at a time.

3. Once meringue forms soft peaks, about 1 minute, add vanilla and/or food coloring, if using. Continue to whisk until meringue holds stiff peaks, about 8–10 minutes.

CONTINUED

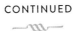

4. Transfer meringue to a piping bag fitted with a large star tip. Press tip to a prepared baking sheet and hold for a second as meringue forms upward, then stop applying pressure and lift quickly to create a slightly curved tip. Repeat with remaining meringue.

5. Bake 90 minutes until meringues are dry to the touch. Turn off oven and leave meringues in closed oven another 1 hour. They are done when they pull off parchment paper very easily. Store at room temperature in a closed container for up to 5 days.

MERINGUES

Any meringue recipe requires that you weigh your ingredients using a kitchen scale. As scales come in all shapes, sizes, and price ranges, it's easy (and essential in some cases) to have one in your kitchen. The key to successful meringue is to ensure that your whites do not come into contact with any fats. Clean your bowl and spatula well before starting, and make sure no yolks sneak into your mixture.

Whistledown Dippers

There is nothing quite as enticing as the improprieties and misconduct worthy of scathing reports by Lady Whistledown's pen. While you are hypnotized and entranced by the sordid stories, munch away at these little teatime dippers. They are perfect dipped in banana pudding, your afternoon tea, or perhaps ratafia in the evening hours.

MAKES 18 DIPPERS

1 cup all-purpose flour
$^1/_2$ teaspoon baking powder
4 large eggs
$^1/_2$ cup granulated sugar, divided

1. Preheat oven to 375°F. Line a baking sheet with parchment paper.

2. In a medium bowl, sift together flour and baking powder and set aside.

3. Separate egg whites and yolks into two small bowls. Add $^1/_4$ cup sugar to yolks and beat until pale in color.

4. In a stand mixer fitted with a whisk attachment, or using a hand mixer, beat egg whites until soft peaks form, about 3 minutes. Slowly add remaining $^1/_4$ cup sugar to whites, continuing to beat until firm, glossy peaks form, about 8 minutes.

5. Using a spatula, gently fold yolk mixture into egg white mixture, taking care not to deflate whites. Gently fold in flour mixture and transfer to a piping bag or large sealable bag with a corner cut off for a tip. Pipe eighteen long, thin lines of batter onto baking sheet.

6. Bake 10–15 minutes depending on desired firmness. Allow to cool before eating, about 20 minutes.

DIPPERS

Dippers are outrageously delicious and elegant bite-sized cookies or cookie sandwiches full of your favorite filling. The ton might have indulged with a chocolate or pecan filling. Today you might add hazelnut spread between these finger cookies for the perfect sandwich. Whatever the era or palate, dippers promise to satisfy.

Marina's Letter Cookies

Waiting for happy ever after is a tedious affair, and to have all hopes dashed by a letter of rejection is as cruel a fate as any. And yet Marina, facing new fortunes, has rid herself of the plight of pity in a manner both abrupt and dubious. These jam-filled cookies bake as quickly as her fortune, though they are perhaps sweeter.

**MAKES 12 HEART COOKIES
OR 24 TRIANGLE COOKIES**

2 large eggs
$\frac{1}{2}$ cup granulated sugar
$\frac{1}{2}$ cup canola (or other neutral) oil
1 teaspoon vanilla extract
1 teaspoon baking powder
1 teaspoon salt
$2\frac{1}{2}$ cups all-purpose flour
1 (13-ounce) jar strawberry jam

1. In a stand mixer fitted with a paddle attachment, beat eggs and sugar. Add oil and vanilla and mix until combined. Add baking powder, salt, and flour and mix until a dough forms.

2. Remove dough from mixer and knead into a ball. Cover with plastic wrap and refrigerate 1 hour.

3. Preheat oven to 350°F. Line two baking sheets with parchment paper.

4. Roll out chilled dough on a clean, lightly floured surface to about ¼" thick.

5. To make heart cookies, use a 3" heart-shaped cutter to cut out twenty-four heart shapes, rerolling excess dough and cutting as you go. Fill middle of each heart with ½ teaspoon jam and then gently place a second heart on top, using the blunt end of a chopstick or fork to seal edges.

6. To make triangle cookies, cut dough into twenty-four 2½" squares. Place 1 teaspoon jam into center of each. Fold one end to the other, creating a triangle shape. Press down to seal edges. If desired, use small cookie cutters to make decorative shapes out of any excess dough to place on each cookie.

7. Place on prepared baking sheets and bake 20 minutes or until edges begin to slightly brown. Let cool slightly before serving; the jam inside will be quite hot.

SPOILER ALERT

In the book *To Sir Phillip, with Love*, Marina is a distant cousin of the Bridgertons who marries Sir Phillip Crane. She ends up dying, and Eloise (of all people) and Sir Phillip fall in love.

First Bloom Mini Muffins with Blue Buttercream Frosting

When the hydrangeas are in full bloom, it is time to celebrate
with blue buttercream: a truly euphoric frosting that dances upon the palate
like young newlyweds on their honeymoon. These mini treats should be
served alongside an appropriate floral arrangement and perhaps
adorned with sugared edible flowers.

MAKES 24 MINI MUFFINS

For Mini Muffins
¼ cup unsalted butter, softened
½ cup granulated sugar
2 large eggs
⅓ cup whole milk
1 teaspoon vanilla extract
1½ teaspoons baking powder
½ teaspoon salt
1½ cups all-purpose flour, divided

For Buttercream Frosting
4 cups confectioners' sugar
1 cup unsalted butter, softened
2 teaspoons vanilla extract
1 teaspoon blue food coloring
1 tablespoon whole milk

CONTINUED

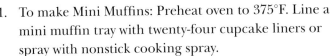

1. To make Mini Muffins: Preheat oven to 375°F. Line a mini muffin tray with twenty-four cupcake liners or spray with nonstick cooking spray.

2. In a stand mixer fitted with a paddle attachment, beat butter and granulated sugar together. Add eggs, milk, and vanilla and mix. Add dry ingredients and mix until just combined.

3. Scoop batter into a piping bag and pipe into prepared muffin cups until ¾ full.

4. Bake 12 minutes or until a toothpick comes out clean. Remove muffins from tray and allow to cool on a cooling rack 15 minutes.

5. To make Buttercream Frosting: In a large bowl, mix confectioners' sugar, butter, and vanilla until fully incorporated.

6. Slowly add food coloring, mixing until fully combined. Slowly add milk while stirring until frosting consistency is reached. If too thick, add more milk.

7. Add Buttercream Frosting to a piping bag with desired frosting tip and pipe onto muffins.

MINI MUFFINS

Embodying the "too much is never enough" philosophy of the Regency period, these Mini Muffins only add to the delicious overindulgence of teatime. The blue Buttercream Frosting matches Eloise's dress, but she pretends to be too sophisticated to notice. However, her siblings raise eyebrows as she puts several muffins on her plate and retreats back to the sofa to write in her journal.

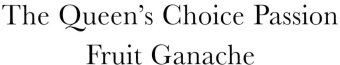

The Queen's Choice Passion Fruit Ganache

Like the young lords and ladies, festooned between the pillars of high society for all to see and judge, a ganache, too, bears outsized scrutiny from society— for folks do like to chatter and nitpick like scavenging birds. Know that your teatime treats are safe from ridicule with this lovely ganache.

MAKES 1 CUP

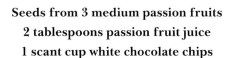

Seeds from 3 medium passion fruits
2 tablespoons passion fruit juice
1 scant cup white chocolate chips

1. In a food processor, pulse together fruit and fruit juice. Using a small sieve, remove seeds. Set mixture aside.

2. In a small microwave-safe bowl, heat chocolate chips on high in 30-second intervals, stirring well after each cook time until chips are melted.

3. In a separate small microwave-safe bowl, microwave passion fruit mixture on high in 25-second intervals until hot.

4. Stir passion fruit mixture into melted chocolate until well mixed. Refrigerate mixture 1 hour until almost firm but still able to be piped.

....

PASSION FRUIT

Passion fruit, from the Latin *passiflora*, was originally linked by missionaries in the New World to the passion of Christ and his crucifixion when converting indigenous peoples. During the Regency, however, passion was directed exclusively at one's object of desire. This ganache, lovers hope, will inspire the passion of one's heart's desire.

Marry for Love Mini Muffins with Cinnamon Streusel

May your love for these muffins be as pure as that of the late
Lord Bridgerton and Lady Bridgerton. For in the end, our beloved
ton seeks true love and, perhaps, a palace. Serve these on a platter for
all to see, perhaps to catch the eye of a reputable lord.

MAKES 24 MINI MUFFINS

1½ cups plus 6 tablespoons all-purpose flour, divided
½ cup plus 4 tablespoons granulated sugar, divided
2 tablespoons canola (or other neutral) oil
1 tablespoon ground cinnamon
¼ cup unsalted butter, softened
2 large eggs
⅓ cup whole milk
1 teaspoon vanilla extract
1½ teaspoons baking powder
½ teaspoon salt

1. Preheat oven to 375°F and line a mini muffin tray with twenty-four cupcake liners or spray with nonstick cooking spray.

2. In a small bowl, mix 6 tablespoons flour, 4 tablespoons sugar, oil, and cinnamon with a fork. Set aside.

3. In a stand mixer fitted with a paddle attachment, beat butter and remaining ½ cup sugar together.

4. Once combined, add eggs, milk, and vanilla. Add baking powder, salt, and remaining 1½ cups flour and stir until just combined.

5. Scoop batter into a piping bag and pipe into prepared muffin cups until ¾ full. Spoon cinnamon-sugar mixture over muffins and bake 12 minutes or until a toothpick inserted in center comes out clean. Allow to cool to 10 minutes before serving.

. . . .

STREUSEL

Too much is never enough when it comes to love and sweets! These mini muffins call out for streusel—the crumbly, sugary coating that tops them—as Daphne calls for Simon in the long summer evenings following their outings.

The Modiste's Mini Macarons

Like everyone in Bridgerton, Madame Delacroix has her own share of secrets, such as the source of her alluring and exotic accent. But who has time to dillydally with such hearsay when the next ball is at hand and the Featheringtons are in need of new dresses (since of course it is unimaginable to wear the same dress twice)? Macarons, like some in the ton, are unforgiving. Measure ingredients on your kitchen scale.

MAKES ABOUT 22 MACARONS

95 grams almond flour
85 grams confectioners' sugar
66 grams aged (refrigerated 2 days) egg whites, room temperature
¼ teaspoon cream of tartar
60 grams superfine granulated sugar
A few drops gel food coloring (optional)
1 batch The Queen's Choice Passion Fruit Ganache (see recipe in this chapter)

1. Prepare a piping bag with a round tip. Line three baking sheets with silicone baking mats or parchment paper.

2. In a medium bowl, sift together almond flour and confectioners' sugar, discarding or pulverizing any larger clumps. In a food processor, pulverize flour mixture and sift again. Don't push through any large pieces. Set aside.

3. In a stand mixer fitted with a whisk attachment, beat egg whites until foamy, about 2 minutes, then add cream of tartar and granulated sugar one small spoonful at a time. When soft peaks form after another 2 minutes, add food coloring, if using.

4. Turn mixer to second-highest speed and continue beating until firm, glossy peaks form, about 8 minutes. Meringue is ready when it clumps up in whisk and stays put if bowl is turned upside down.

CONTINUED

5. Carefully fold flour mixture into meringue, scraping spatula around the sides, folding over, and occasionally cutting through mixture. Continue until batter begins to flow smoothly. Batter should run off spatula in a ribbonlike stream when ready.

6. Transfer mixture immediately to piping bag (if using parchment paper, dab a pea-sized amount of batter under each corner so it won't blow around in oven). Holding bag perpendicular to baking sheet, pipe 1" circles 2" apart.

7. Slam each tray down on counter twice to help pop any air bubbles and then use a bamboo skewer, butter knife, or the back of a spoon to smooth any peaks. Let macaron shells rest 30 minutes or until matte and no longer sticky.

8. Preheat oven to 300°F.

9. Bake macarons, one tray at a time, in center rack of oven, rotating halfway through baking time, approximately 13 minutes. To test for doneness, touch a macaron shell gently: It should not wiggle. Transfer parchment or mat to a cooling rack and allow macarons to cool entirely, about 45 minutes.

10. To fill shells, pair each shell with one the same size, and flip one over. Using the same small round piping tip, pipe The Queen's Choice Passion Fruit Ganache onto flipped shells and then sandwich with remaining shells. Cover and refrigerate overnight before serving.

MACARONS

Macarons, like much of the finest food of the Regency, were inspired or created by French chefs. These glorious macarons, as fussy as they are beautiful, only gain in reputation because (like many of the ladies in the ton) they require special, loving attention. Yet, their admirers assert, they are very much worth the effort. With proper measuring, and some patience, you'll produce the characteristic smooth and shiny shells with perfectly formed little feet. The result is chewy on the inside with a satisfying crunch on the outside.

Pear and Apple Chips

Convert your daily fruit into priceless gems. These crispy, semitranslucent fruit chips are as delicate as an evening gown—with the snap of Cressida's snarl. Take these with you for a stroll through the gardens or use them to decorate your favorite cake.

MAKES 2 CUPS

2 cups water
2 cups granulated sugar
1 medium Bosc pear, peeled, cored, and cut into ¼"-thick slices
1 medium Gala apple, peeled, cored, and cut into ¼"-thick slices
1 teaspoon ground cinnamon (optional)

1. Preheat oven to 200°F. Line two baking sheets with parchment paper.

2. In a small saucepan over high heat, bring water and sugar to a boil. Once a syrup has formed, about 5 minutes, add fruit slices, then carefully remove after 30 seconds.

3. Pat slices with a paper towel and lay out in a single layer on baking sheets. Sprinkle with cinnamon, if using. Bake 2 hours, turning halfway through. Allow to cool 5 minutes before serving.

. . . .

MANDOLINE

The great kitchens during the Regency had little need for a mandoline to help slice their fruits and vegetables. After all, they had scullery maids and kitchen maids to do this work. Nowadays, kitchen help usually comes in the form of electrical appliances and must-have gadgets, such as the invaluable mandoline that slices produce into thin, perfect shapes in just a few minutes. There's no need to put up with the grumblings of the staff either!

Rumor-Stirring Blueberry Lavender Fizz

What goes better with teatime scones than a delicious fruity drink?
This nonalcoholic recipe pairs delightfully with good company (and gossip), with its
glorious meringue-like foam that is sure to ruffle Lady Trowbridge's feathers.
Garnish with a fresh lavender flower if your heart desires.

SERVES 1

1 teaspoon dried lavender flowers
1 tablespoon blueberry jam
½ ounce lemon juice
½ ounce lime juice
½ ounce heavy cream
1 large egg white, pasteurized
8–12 ounces cooled sparkling water
1 tablespoon lemon zest

1. Muddle lavender in a cocktail shaker.
2. Add remaining ingredients except sparkling water and lemon zest. Shake vigorously until texture changes to a foam, about 10 seconds.
3. Fill cocktail shaker with ice. Shake 15 seconds or until cocktail is well chilled.
4. Strain into a Collins glass. Top with sparkling water and garnish with lemon zest.

LAVENDER

Not only is lavender a beautiful plant that was used for table decorations, but it was also used during the Regency as a perfume and a medicine because it was thought to help with romance and love. Both men and women of the ton used considerable amounts of perfume, as bathing was not a major part of their hygienic practice.

Spice Trade Biscuits

These fabulous buttery cookies have subtle hints of ginger and cinnamon and go just splendidly with tea and good conversation. This is a great recipe if you intend to use molds. It is customary in great households to have one's own personal family cookie mold! These cookies are suitable for dipping in a sweet wine or ratafia.

MAKES 24 BISCUITS

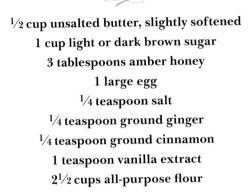

½ **cup unsalted butter, slightly softened**
1 **cup light or dark brown sugar**
3 **tablespoons amber honey**
1 **large egg**
¼ **teaspoon salt**
¼ **teaspoon ground ginger**
¼ **teaspoon ground cinnamon**
1 **teaspoon vanilla extract**
2½ **cups all-purpose flour**

1. Preheat oven to 400°F. Line two baking sheets with parchment paper.

2. In a large bowl, mix together butter, sugar, honey, egg, salt, ginger, cinnamon, and vanilla until fully integrated.

3. Transfer to a stand mixer fitted with a paddle attachment. Mix flour 1 cup at a time until you have a slightly sticky ball. Wrap dough in plastic wrap and refrigerate 2 hours or until cold.

4. On a clean, lightly floured surface, roll out dough to about ¼" thick. Cut out twenty-four shapes with a cookie cutter and press with a mold (lightly dusted with flour) if desired. Excess dough can be rerolled and cut again.

5. Place on prepared baking sheets and bake 10–12 minutes until dark golden brown.

CINNAMON

Cinnamon has been known and prized for thousands of years, considered a spice fit for a king and, of course, a queen. Cinnamon is derived from the bark of a tree, and during the Regency period, the British owned enormous plantations in India to produce this treasured ingredient.

CHAPTER 4

The Grand Banquet

Few pleasures excite the senses as much as the grand banquet, a most celebrated event and the highlight of the day. The table is adorned with gilded dishware of silver and gold, tiered platters, wines, and ratafia. On full display are not only the countless and lavish spreads of roasted game, fish, soups, and pies, but also the hosting family's own pride and dignity! Oh, what a frenzy of wealth, taste, and culture, not to mention the colorful guests. And though the banquet is a most formal event, this is, of course, the Regency, and no menu would be complete without a simmering pot of intrigue, romance, and transgression.

It is customary, of course, that all who attend apply the proper labor and commitment to dressing up: frocks, chemises, and cravats, even if only family members are present. And with guests, well, let's just say the preparations and showmanship know no bounds. Tables are to be bejeweled in a fashion that is both stunning and lavish without being cluttered or crammed—hence the use of tiered platters. All courses for the meal are spread out lavishly except for the soup and the entrées, which must be served hot. It is customary to have two courses of small dishes, and each time one course is finished, the table must be cleared and reset.

Soups

———— ◆ ————

With the hostess seated at the head of the table, the fragrant overture begins with the soup course, brought out first and served hot or cold. Guests mustn't pass up this opportunity to whet the appetite and compliment the hosting party for their grace and remarkable taste. It is also appropriate to hold the spoon in a sideways fashion and use with graceful swoops so as to avoid the appalling indecency of a direct poke into the dish. Take heed not to allow the spoon to touch the bowl either, for this surely will reflect one's inability to maintain composure. Grunts, slurps, and other vulgarities will not be tolerated at such an early stage of the night, though surely, as the evening progresses and the wine flows, exceptions can be made.

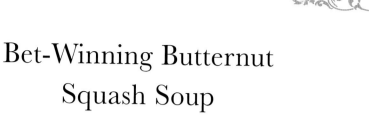

Bet-Winning Butternut Squash Soup

Butternut squash has a lovely nutty flavor and is commonly served in country manors both large and small. Swirl in a bit of Clotted Cream (see recipe in Chapter 2) to catch the eye. Serve alongside roasted root vegetables and a hunted grouse for a charming country dinner.

SERVES 4

1 medium butternut squash, cut lengthwise and seeded

3 tablespoons olive oil

8 medium cloves garlic, peeled

6 large sage leaves, divided

2½ cups beef or vegetable broth

1 cup light cream

1½ teaspoons kosher salt

1¼ teaspoons harissa powder, divided

4 tablespoons sunflower seeds

1. Preheat oven to 350°F.

2. Place squash halves in a large ungreased baking dish cut-side up. Drizzle oil into cavities where seeds were removed and top oil with garlic cloves. Add 4 sage leaves to cavities.

3. Bake 1 hour uncovered until squash turns dark red. In a small saucepan gently heat broth over medium heat until it begins to boil. Set aside to cool 5 minutes.

CONTINUED

4. Gently scoop out squash, including garlic and sage, from skin and place in a blender. Add cream, broth, salt, and 1 teaspoon harissa and blend until creamy, about 1 minute.

5. Transfer to four medium bowls, stir in salt, and garnish with sunflower seeds and remaining 2 sage leaves and remaining ¼ teaspoon harissa.

BUTTERNUT SQUASH

Did you know that butternut squash is a fruit? Originally from the Americas, the European colonizers brought this squash back to the Old World. The Regency-era cooks cooked it in various ways—roasted, baked, and in soups— to bring out its sweet, nutty flavor. The skin and seeds of this fruit can also be eaten and are especially good if roasted.

Refined Chestnut Soup

*Here we have a hearty gentleman's soup, one not easily swayed by
seduction or levigated by lust. This soup is just plain delightful, rich in character
and virtue, just like Colin Bridgerton. This is a noble and soothing soup,
perfect on its own or as a course in a larger banquet.*

SERVES 2

6 tablespoons unsalted butter

1 large yellow onion, peeled and diced

1 small stalk celery, diced

1 small carrot, peeled and diced

1 small leek, diced

6 medium cloves garlic

10 ounces roasted chestnuts

4 cups chicken broth

½ teaspoon ground fennel

1 small pasilla chile, seeded

3 large bay leaves

1 teaspoon kosher salt

⅓ teaspoon ground white pepper

1 cup heavy cream

½ cup sour cream

1 tablespoon finely chopped chives

1. In a medium pot over medium heat, melt butter then add onion, celery, carrot, leek, and garlic and cook until tender, about 10 minutes.

2. Add chestnuts, broth, fennel, pasilla, and bay leaves and simmer over medium heat 20 minutes to reduce broth.

3. Add salt and white pepper and simmer 1 minute. Add heavy cream and cook several minutes until thick enough to coat the back of a spoon.

4. Remove and discard pasilla and bay leaves and let cool 10 minutes.

5. Pour into a blender and blend until smooth. Serve hot topped with sour cream and chives.

AMERICAN CHESTNUT TREES

American chestnut trees used to dominate the eastern United States
and were some of the largest trees, with trunk diameters reaching 10 feet!
Sadly, they became endangered around the early 1900s due to a series of
diseases. There is thought to be only a handful left. Currently, there are
efforts underway to introduce blight-resistant varieties.

Future-Securing Lobster Bisque

*The life of the beau monde is like a simmering pot of ambition,
a stew that, if executed correctly, ensures one's future successes. But be
careful, for the slightest misdeed could scald you. A bisque such as this one
will ensure your name is forever marked by triumph.*

SERVES 6

3 large lobster tails

1½ tablespoons olive oil

1½ tablespoons unsalted butter

1 small yellow onion, peeled and finely chopped

4 medium cloves garlic, peeled and finely chopped

1 medium red bell pepper, seeded and finely chopped

2 medium stalks celery, finely chopped

1 cube fish bouillon

2 tablespoons all-purpose flour

½ cup white wine

2 tablespoons tomato paste

4 cups fish broth

2 tablespoons finely chopped fresh tarragon, divided

1 teaspoon kosher salt

1 teaspoon ground black pepper

½ cup heavy cream (optional)

1. Fill a large pot ¾ full with water and boil lobster tails over high heat, about 10–12 minutes, until they turn red and are cooked through. Internal temperature should reach at least 145°F. Remove from water and set aside to cool, about 10 minutes. Remove meat from shells and chop. Set aside.

2. In a large heavy skillet over low heat, heat oil and butter. Add onion and garlic and cook, stirring often, for 5 minutes. Add bell pepper and celery and cook, stirring often, 5 minutes or until tender. Crumble in fish bouillon and mix well.

3. Add flour and stir constantly 3 minutes until cooked. Slowly add wine and stir vigorously. Add tomato paste.

4. Slowly add fish broth, stirring gently until it begins to thicken, about 2–3 minutes. Add 1 tablespoon tarragon, salt, and black pepper.

5. Add ⅔ chopped lobster to skillet. Add cream, if desired, and cook another 2 minutes.

6. Remove from heat and carefully pour into a blender. Blend until smooth. Pour into six medium bowls and garnish with remaining lobster and remaining 1 tablespoon tarragon.

. . . .

LOBSTER BISQUE

The lobster bisque that we know today came into existence at the time of the Regency. Originally a fisherman's soup made from crustacean shells, it developed into a luxury dish fit for the ton's finest table. While most recipes call for the lobster shells to be boiled separately—after the meat has been cooked and removed from the tail—to add to the broth, the beau monde does not think the difference in taste justifies the additional labor.

Head-Turning Coconut Shrimp Soup

This soup showers its brilliance upon all lucky guests like a ray of sunshine. It uses the rare coconut as a bowl, so only those with means are able to afford such refinement and exotic luxuries. Coconut soup would truly have been a majestic experience.

SERVES 6

1 small Yukon Gold potato

6 tablespoons vegetable oil, divided

1 large leek, diced

10 medium cloves garlic, peeled, diced, and divided

$1\frac{1}{2}$ pounds shrimp, peeled and deveined

$1\frac{1}{2}$ teaspoons kosher salt

1 teaspoon ground black pepper

3 cups unsweetened coconut milk

6 tablespoons red curry paste

1 tablespoon fresh grated ginger

1 bunch (about $\frac{1}{2}$ cup) fresh cilantro, washed and destemmed

1 large ripe mango, peeled and diced into $\frac{1}{3}$" cubes

1. Add potato to a small pot of water and bring to a boil over high heat. Lower heat to medium and simmer until fork-tender, about 20–30 minutes. Remove from heat to cool, about 10 minutes.

2. In a small saucepan over medium heat, add 3 tablespoons oil, leek, and 6 cloves garlic. Cook 10 minutes until fragrant and leek is soft. Set aside to cool, about 5 minutes.

3. In a large saucepan over high heat, add remaining 3 tablespoons oil, shrimp, remaining 4 cloves garlic, salt, and pepper. Cook 5 minutes until shrimp become pink and reach an internal temperature of 165°.

CONTINUED

4. In a food processor, add leek mixture, potato, and coconut milk and purée.

5. Pour purée into a medium saucepan over low heat and add curry paste and ginger. Cook 2 minutes, stirring often. Remove from heat. Pour purée into coconut halves or individual soup bowls.

6. Chop shrimp to desired size and mix in with purée. Garnish soup with cilantro and mango.

COCONUT

Coconut is actually a fruit, not a nut. The word coco is slang for "head" in Spanish and Portuguese. While serving this soup in the coconut shell must have been an exhilarating sight, those of us without scullery maids might consider using canned coconut milk and serving this soup in beautiful bowls. This presentation, too, will impress guests and enhance reputations in social circles.

Chilled Pea Soup Fit for a Lord

This beautiful soup is most refreshing on a hot and stuffy day.
It is light enough to be quite suitable for teatime or as a soup course at dinner.
Its creaminess is accented perfectly with a touch of white pepper and lemon juice.

SERVES 4

1/4 medium red onion, peeled and thinly sliced

4 tablespoons fresh lemon juice, divided

1 tablespoon granulated sugar

2 cups chicken broth, boiled then chilled

2 cups frozen peas

2 tablespoons plain yogurt

3 tablespoons extra-virgin olive oil

1/2 teaspoon kosher salt

1/2 teaspoon ground white pepper

2 teaspoons lemon zest

1 tablespoon minced fresh tarragon

1. Place onion slices in a small bowl with 3 tablespoons lemon juice and sugar. Let sit 30 minutes.

2. In a medium pot bring broth to a boil. Once boiling add peas and remove from heat. Cool 15 minutes, then pour into a blender. Add 2 tablespoons yogurt, oil, and remaining 1 tablespoon lemon juice and blend until smooth. Slowly add salt and white pepper and continue blending until fully incorporated, about 30 seconds.

3. Pour into four serving bowls and add lemon zest. Garnish with tarragon.

. . . .

PEAS

Garden peas were cultivated during the Regency era and considered a delicacy. They required a fair amount of work, as their tough outer skins needed to be removed by scullery maids before the cook or chef could work their magic.

Well-Matched Sausage and Mushroom Soup

When dreary days are upon us, as is quite usually the case in London, the perfect pairing of sausage and mushroom in this delicious soup will lift the spirits with its warm, hearty complexion as well as its high levels of vitamin D. This is a soup Mrs. Colson might make for the Duke of Hastings, with earthy spices that play nicely with some crème fraîche or Clotted Cream.

SERVES 4

2 tablespoons canola (or other neutral) oil

1 large Vidalia onion,
peeled and finely chopped

16 ounces shitake mushrooms, thinly sliced

8 ounces pork sausage

6 medium cloves garlic, peeled and minced

1 teaspoon ground cumin

1 tablespoon ground ancho chile

8 ounces tomato paste

4 cups beef stock

1 tablespoon fresh grated ginger

Juice from $\frac{1}{2}$ medium lemon

4 tablespoons crème fraîche or Clotted Cream (see recipe in Chapter 2)

4 slices lemon

1. In a large saucepan over medium heat, add oil and onion. Cook until onion is caramelized, about 15 minutes. Add mushrooms and cook 10–15 minutes to remove excess water. Add sausage and cook 10 minutes or until internal temperature reaches 145°F.

2. And garlic, cumin, ancho chile, tomato paste, and stock. Cook 20 minutes until reduced by ¼. Add ginger and lemon juice and mix well.

3. Divide into four medium bowls and garnish each with a dollop of crème fraîche or Clotted Cream and slice of lemon.

MARIE-ANTOINE CARÊME

While the most famous chef of the Regency era, Marie-Antoine Carême, put mushrooms to exquisite use in his recipes, he probably did not know all the amazing things we now know about mushrooms. Varieties such as Chaga and reishi are known to reduce cancerous tumors, while others are capable of breaking down plastics and other toxic materials.

Heritage Mushroom Cream of Barley

Not all secrets are perilous. This heavily guarded recipe of the Clyvedon kitchen is simply too good to keep secret. It has been such a favorite of the former duchess that it is considered a family heirloom. Always a hit with guests, it is hot and fulfilling, and it brings immense satisfaction to all who get to experience it.

SERVES 4

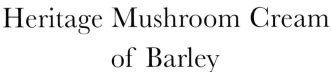

1½ cups pearled barley

1½ cups bone or mushroom broth

2 tablespoons unsalted butter

1 tablespoon olive oil

1 cup finely diced shallots

16 ounces maitake or cremini mushrooms, sliced

1 medium stalk celery, finely chopped

½ cup all-purpose flour

1 teaspoon fresh thyme leaves

1 cup sour cream

2 tablespoons finely chopped chives

1. In a small pot over low heat, add barley and broth and boil until barley is soft, about 30 minutes.

2. Add butter, oil, shallots, mushrooms, and celery to a medium Dutch oven. Cook over medium heat until tender, 10–15 minutes. Mix in flour and cook an additional 1 minute.

3. Pour barley and broth in Dutch oven and stir. Add thyme. Cook 1–2 minutes longer until thyme softens. Allow mixture to cool completely, about 30 minutes, then mix in sour cream.

4. Spoon into four medium bowls and garnish with chives.

· · · · · · · · · ·

BARLEY

In the Regency period, barley, the oldest cultivated grain, was a significant part of the whiskey trade and dominated the beer industry. John Barleycorn was a mythic man from British and Scottish folk song representing the grain grown through the summer, cut down in the fall, and reborn as whiskey and beer!

Vegetables and Leafy Greens

———— ◆ ————

Though vegetables perhaps are not the center of attention, any illustrious and complete meal is sure to have several vegetable courses. Obviously, it is customary to serve these dishes with heaps of browned butter to add some weight and personality. But times are changing, and the pillars of tradition begin to waver: The Regency is full of daring ambition!

It is commonly known that older generations would often look upon the leafy greens with suspicion, as many were considered either medicinal or poisonous, and therefore not appropriate or appealing for the evening's guests. Yet those were the old times, and today's ton really does fancy the lightness and alluring tastes of fresh vegetables from the countryside. And with all the traveled folk, well, let's just say they have seen and experienced a vast array of vegetable delights from across Europe as well as the colonies. Even Colin suggests bringing back tomato plants from Greece as a gift for Marina, assuming of course nothing dastardly occurs before he takes his leave.

The Prince Regent's Potato Plumpers

The young prince regent is getting "plumper by the day" according to her highness, the queen. And it's no surprise since he has a rapturous appetite and a fondness for this dish of perfectly sculpted potatoes. They are crowned with a golden, crunchy top while maintaining a soft, buttery interior. They are handsome and composed, as any potato on the table must be!

SERVES 4

½ cup unsalted butter, divided

2 large Idaho potatoes, as tubular as possible, ends removed, peeled, halved lengthwise

2 sprigs fresh rosemary, divided

½ teaspoon paprika

1 cup bone broth

1 teaspoon sea salt

½ teaspoon ground black pepper

1. Preheat oven to 300°F.
2. In a large oven-safe pan over low heat, add 1 tablespoon butter and place potatoes cut-side up. Gently cook 5–6 minutes until golden brown.
3. Flip potatoes and add remaining 7 tablespoons butter, 1 sprig rosemary, and paprika. Cook until butter starts to brown, about 5 minutes, then add broth.
4. Place in oven and bake 30 minutes. Season with salt, pepper, and needles from remaining sprig rosemary before serving.

....

PAPRIKA

Chefs during the Regency period used paprika. The paprika you know is a spice made up of various ground chiles and milder peppers that originated in the New World. However, the version Regency chefs knew likely came from the Turkish and Hungarian variations of paprika. It adds a wonderful red color to foods that livens up any table, from the prince's potatoes down to the kitchen staff's goulash.

Archibald's Indebted Asparagus

Like the gambler who deals in hope, so, too, does the eligible ton during the social season, for time is of the essence, and one has only so many chances to rise in rank. These little gems are a sure bet and will adorn the family silver nicely with crunchy garlic. For an even more esteemed dish, drizzle with Aged Vinaigrette (see Steamy Artichokes recipe in this chapter).

SERVES 4

3 tablespoons olive oil
1 pound asparagus, bottom 1" removed
3 medium cloves garlic, peeled and sliced
1 teaspoon sea salt
1 teaspoon coarse black pepper

1. In a large skillet over medium-low heat, add oil and asparagus and gently cook until asparagus begins to soften, about 5 minutes.

2. Increase heat to medium-high, add garlic, and cook until garlic and asparagus are golden and crispy, about 3 minutes.

3. Remove from heat and sprinkle with salt and pepper, then serve.

GAMBLING

Gambling was a lucrative pastime and quite on-brand for the Regency's tendencies for debauchery. It was not uncommon for lords to gamble away their estates, though there were some unofficial rules meant to keep the lands within the aristocracy. Since only landowners could vote, laws could protect them if they lost a bet to someone of a lower class.

The Dandy's Superb
Tomato Tartare

Sometimes a dandy with indigestion prefers something on the light side. This tartare is light and refreshing while at the same time as satisfying as steak. It's been said that there are some who do not eat meat at all (gasp!), and if you are ever to entertain one of these odd fellows, do try this. Note: This dish can easily be made into a salad by adding mixed greens around the edge of the plate with an Aged Vinaigrette (see Steamy Artichokes recipe in this chapter).

SERVES 4

8 large, ripe heirloom tomatoes, diced

3 tablespoons olive oil

2 sprigs fresh rosemary

1 tablespoon capers

4 ($\frac{1}{3}$-ounce) fresh mozzarella balls

2 teaspoons sea salt

2 teaspoons ground black pepper

$\frac{1}{2}$ cup microgreens (either pea shoots, basil, or mustard greens)

1. Place 1 diced tomato in a piece of cheesecloth. Over the sink, strain liquid out of tomato. Repeat with remaining tomatoes. Place in a large bowl in refrigerator to cool 1 hour.

2. In a small saucepan over medium-low heat, heat oil. Simmer rosemary sprigs until crunchy, about 5 minutes. Remove from oil and set aside. Allow oil to cool, about 1 minute.

CONTINUED

3. Transfer oil to a small container and refrigerate 1 hour. Once cold, mix oil with tomatoes and capers in a medium bowl.

4. Divide tartare mixture and form into discs about 1" high on four small plates. Garnish each with $\frac{1}{2}$ sprig crunchy rosemary and 1 mozzarella ball in center. Top with salt and pepper. Place microgreens around edges and cover with chilled rosemary oil.

. . . .

TOMATOES

Tomatoes are another of the many foods that the explorers brought from their contact with the Aztecs in the New World. Tomatoes are actually fruits (specifically berries), not vegetables. While the Regency ton knew about tomatoes, many of the older lords and ladies avoided them, considering them unhealthy. The younger generation, of course, knew better, and considered Tomato Tartare a daring and delicious dish.

Colin's Favorite Corn Cakes

This is a gentleman's cake. It is a handsome and savory cake that dresses up rather suitably with Clotted Cream (see recipe in Chapter 2) and berries at breakfast or with meats, vegetables, and gravy at dinner. It's dense, and it holds up well, making it sensible for plating and as a base for layering other goodies on top.

SERVES 8

1½ cups cornmeal
1¾ cups all-purpose flour
1 tablespoon herbes de Provence
1 teaspoon kosher salt
½ cup water
½ cup canola (or other neutral) oil
2 large eggs
1 cup corn kernels (frozen or fresh)

1. In a large bowl, mix cornmeal, flour, herbes de Provence, and salt.

2. In a medium bowl, mix water, oil, and eggs. Stir well. Stir in corn kernels and pour into dry mixture. Mix thoroughly. Batter should be slightly sticky.

3. Roll out aluminum foil and place batter on top. Form batter into a tube about 3"–4" thick and 10" long. Roll tightly in foil, sealing ends. Boil 45 minutes.

4. To serve, remove foil and gently cut into 1" slices.

....

REGENCY ETIQUETTE

The cast of *Bridgerton* had to participate in an intensive six-week training course prior to shooting so they could learn the proper etiquette of the Regency era. This included learning all the dances, how to ride horses, and, of course, how to act like proper ladies and gentlemen.

Steamy Artichokes

The Duke and the Duchess of Hastings love eating artichokes (among other activities!), but they cannot agree on the best dipping sauce. Daphne prefers the Tarragon Lemon Aioli, while Simon favors the Aged Vinaigrette. Let's have you decide your favorite with these delightful options.

SERVES 4

For Artichokes
4 large artichokes

For Tarragon Lemon Aioli
$1/4$ cup chopped fresh tarragon
$1/2$ cup chopped fresh cilantro
2 medium cloves garlic, peeled
$1/2$ teaspoon salt
$1/3$ cup olive oil
1 tablespoon lemon juice
1 large egg yolk, pasteurized

For Aged Vinaigrette
4 tablespoons extra-virgin olive oil
1 tablespoon aged balsamic vinegar
1 medium clove garlic, peeled and pressed
$1/4$ teaspoon Dijon mustard
$1/16$ teaspoon salt
$1/16$ teaspoon ground black pepper

1. To make Artichokes: Remove outer leaves, cut 1" off tops and $1/2$" off stems. Cut in half lengthwise and scoop out and discard hairy fibers in center. Place artichokes in a steamer basket in a large pot with enough water to almost reach basket. Bring water to a boil over high heat. Once boiling, lower heat to low and check to make sure there is water still in pot. Cook artichokes 30–40 minutes until outer leaves pull out easily. Remove from heat and cover while making sauces.

2. To make Tarragon Lemon Aioli: In a blender, add tarragon, cilantro, garlic, and salt, and slowly add oil with blender on high speed. Slowly add lemon juice, still blending. Add egg yolk. Blend until creamy. Store in a medium sealed container in the refrigerator up to 1 week.

3. To make Aged Vinaigrette: Combine all ingredients in a medium bowl and whisk, or shake in a medium sealed container. Vinaigrette will last up to 5 days in refrigerator. Whisk immediately before serving.

ARTICHOKES

The ton loves artichokes, which have been associated with nobility since Henry VIII grew the thorny thistle in the royal garden. The heart and the fleshy parts of the leaves closest to it are delicious—especially served with sauces or grilled. But beware of the spiny tips and the choke. Very high in antioxidants, artichokes are as good for you as they are delicious!

The Footman's Finest
Roasted Vegetables

*Like swirling young couples on the dance floor, these vegetables together
make for quite the celebration. With a multitude of colors and textures like our
favorite couples, this dish is deceivingly simple. The high heat will slightly
caramelize the vegetables, giving them a delicious taste. The kitchen staff
can prepare this in minutes, but its lingering joy will remain for hours.*

SERVES 4

1/2 cup chopped peeled carrots

1/2 cup chopped peeled sweet potato

1/2 cup chopped peeled parsnips

1/2 cup chopped peeled beets

1/2 cup chopped peeled red onion

1/2 cup chopped Brussels sprouts

1/2 cup peeled whole garlic cloves

1 tablespoon za'atar

3 sprigs fresh rosemary, divided

2 tablespoons extra-virgin olive oil

1/2 teaspoon salt

1/2 teaspoon ground black pepper

1 tablespoon lemon zest

CONTINUED

1. Preheat oven to 450°F.

2. In a large ungreased baking dish, add all vegetables, za'atar, and 2 sprigs rosemary. Drizzle with oil and sprinkle with salt and pepper. Toss.

3. Bake uncovered 45 minutes, turning mixture every 15 minutes during baking. Once baked, sprinkle with lemon zest and garnish with remaining rosemary sprig.

. . . .

ZA'ATAR

Za'atar, an Arabic word, is a Middle Eastern combination of herbs—several varieties of thyme, oregano, marjoram, and other herbs found in the Mediterranean region. There are many variations of za'atar—some mixed with sumac, sesame seeds, hyssop, and other plants and herbs. Its fresh, nutty flavor adds a delightful tang to many meats, fish, and vegetables.

Dignified Delicata Squash

Nothing in Bridgerton is safe from the stinging pen of Lady Whistledown. And even on the loftiest perch of society, one must sometimes play one's ace. For the higher one's station, the greater the fall from grace. This is a delightfully easy dish for your social repertoire. Top with seasonal herbs or a spice blend like za'atar to put on a real show.

SERVES 4

1 large delicata squash, seeded, cut into 1" -thick circles

8 medium cloves garlic, peeled

4 tablespoons olive oil

1 teaspoon herbes de Provence

1 teaspoon sea salt

1 teaspoon ground black pepper

1. Preheat oven to 400°F.

2. Lay squash circles on an ungreased baking sheet with 1–2 cloves of garlic on each circle. Drizzle with oil, then sprinkle with herbes de Provence, salt, and pepper.

3. Bake 45 minutes or until just beginning to blister. Allow to cool 10 minutes before serving.

. . . .

DELICATA SQUASH

Delicata squash, as its name implies, is the most delicate of all the squash. It does well in warm weather and is easy to grow, but it is less sturdy than its heartier cousins like butternut or acorn squash. Baked in the oven, the delicata squash has an exquisite, nutty flavor. The rind is delicious and crunchy as well when baked.

Potato Mash with the Staff's Secret Salt

Behind every great meal, there is a great cook. And behind every great cook, there is a great secret! For who knows better the gossip and whispers of these darkened chambers than those in the service of maintaining them? Even the lowest of kitchen servants—the scullery maid—picks up a thing or two working in the presence of the great chefs who cook for the ton.

SERVES 6

For Potatoes
2 pounds whole Yukon Gold potatoes
2 teaspoons kosher salt
$\frac{1}{2}$ cup unsalted butter
$\frac{1}{2}$ cup heavy cream
$\frac{1}{2}$ teaspoon Secret Salt (see recipe)

For Secret Salt
$\frac{1}{2}$ cup sea salt
Juice from 1 medium lemon
Zest from 1 medium lemon (optional)

1. To make Potatoes: In a large pot over high heat, add potatoes and enough water to cover them, and bring to a boil. Once boiling, reduce heat to medium and cook potatoes until fork-tender, about 30 minutes.

2. Remove potatoes from water and let cool in a large bowl 30 minutes. Once cooled, gently remove skins with your hands. Discard skins.

3. Add kosher salt, butter, and cream to bowl with potatoes. With a hand mixer (or by hand), combine until potatoes are soft and smooth.

4. To make Secret Salt: Preheat oven to 200°F.

5. In a small bowl, add sea salt. Using a sieve, squeeze in lemon juice and zest (if using) and mix thoroughly.

6. Pour salt mixture onto an ungreased baking sheet and spread evenly. Bake 45 minutes until salt is dry.

7. Sprinkle ⅛ teaspoon or desired amount on potatoes. Remaining Secret Salt can be stored in a small sealed container at room temperature up to 3 months.

· · · · · ·

SALT

Salt was essential for preserving and adding flavor to food before the development of refrigeration. Empires searched for and fought over salt. Salt production and taxes paid for Columbus's explorations and Napoléon's wars. Today, salt is cheap and plentiful. The salt wars are over, but the rivalries to develop the most flavorful salts remain ongoing— the Himalayan pinks; kosher salt; and flaky sea salt that would work marvelously in this recipe.

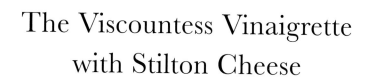

The Viscountess Vinaigrette
with Stilton Cheese

Being of such remarkable grace, Lady Bridgerton surely knows about the finer things in life. The secret to achieving divinity in food is to use only the finest ingredients. This recipe requires strict attention to the quality of the cold-pressed olive oil and the white balsamic vinegar. The greens, too, must be hand-pulled the morning they are to be prepared and brought to town by the fastest carriage. Garnish with edible flowers of your choosing.

SERVES 2

1/2 cup high-quality cold-pressed olive oil

2 tablespoons high-quality white balsamic vinegar

1 clove garlic, peeled and minced

1/2 teaspoon mustard powder

1 teaspoon kosher salt

2 teaspoons ground black pepper

4 ounces fresh, washed mixed greens

3/4 cup walnuts

2 medium ripe pears, sliced or diced

1/3 cup cold, crumbled Stilton cheese

1. Add oil, vinegar, garlic, mustard powder, salt, and pepper to a small container and whisk or shake. Vinaigrette will last up to 5 days in refrigerator. Whisk immediately before serving.

2. In a large bowl, mix together greens, walnuts, pears, and cheese. Toss with dressing and serve immediately.

KETCHUP

Ketchup was a popular sauce during the 1800s, and those with means would make it at home with vinegar, beer, wine, soy sauce, anchovies, and all sorts of other ingredients. Balsamic (meaning "restorative") vinegar comes from crushed Trebbiano grapes, seeds, skins, and stems, creating a "must." This liquid is placed in a series of casks for a minimum of 12 and up to 25 years.

Siena's Spinach with Impassioned Pomegranate Vinaigrette

*For love to bloom, it must have light to grow, lest it die in darkness.
Our poor Siena knows her love with Anthony can never see sunlight and
is destined to perish. Just like Siena's angelic voice, this vinaigrette will
lighten your life and bring love to your heart.*

SERVES 4

1 cup pomegranate juice

$\frac{1}{3}$ cup olive oil

5 teaspoons amber honey

1 tablespoon white balsamic vinegar

1 teaspoon Dijon mustard

$\frac{1}{4}$ teaspoon ground allspice

$\frac{1}{2}$ teaspoon sea salt

$\frac{1}{2}$ teaspoon ground black pepper

1 teaspoon fresh grated ginger

2 tablespoons unsalted butter

4 ($\frac{1}{4}$"-thick) slices sourdough bread, crusts removed, cut into 5" × 2" rectangles

1 large bunch fresh spinach

2 tablespoons sliced toasted almonds

4 tablespoons fresh pomegranate seeds

1. Preheat oven to 400°F. Line a baking sheet with parchment paper.

2. In a small saucepan over low heat, reduce pomegranate juice by half, about 10–15 minutes. Mix in oil, honey, vinegar, mustard, allspice, salt, and pepper and cook an additional 1 minute, mixing constantly. Remove from heat and transfer to a medium bowl. Mix in ginger and allow mixture to cool, about 5 minutes.

3. Butter one side of each bread slice. Connect ends of each slice to make tubes with the buttered side out and attach with a wet toothpick or stainless steel wire. Bake on prepared baking sheet 10–15 minutes until golden brown. Place on a large plate.

4. Toss spinach, almonds, and pomegranate seeds in vinaigrette and serve inside sourdough rings.

. . . .

ROWAN PIERCE

Rowan Pierce is an English-born soprano and opera star who does all the singing for actress Sabrina Bartlett, who plays our beloved Siena Rosso. During the Regency, being an opera singer was considered scandalous since the singers would often have a wealthy man support them in exchange for sex.

Seductively Red Beet Salad with Fennel, Yogurt, and Granola

The choice of which type of beets to use—purple or golden—depends strictly on the table settings and floral arrangements, though the purple variety is sure to stir passions. Fennel pollen is a delightful ingredient that livens up this dish, and if you do not have it in your spice collection, this is a good opportunity to add it.

SERVES 4

1 pound purple and/or golden beets
1 cup plain yogurt
1 cup granola
1 teaspoon fennel pollen or ground fennel seeds
2 cups beet or pea shoot microgreens

1. In a medium pot over high heat, bring enough water to boil to completely cover beets. Add beets and boil until tender, about 20 minutes.

2. Remove beets from water and let cool about 10 minutes. Once cool, gently peel and discard skins. Chop beets into ½" cubes.

3. Add ¼ cup yogurt to a medium plate. With the back of the spoon, spread yogurt across plate like a brush stroke. Gently place ¼ beets on yogurt. Repeat to make four servings. Sprinkle equal amounts granola, fennel pollen or fennel seeds, and microgreens on top of each plate.

. . . .

BEETS

Beets—dark wine red, yellow, white, and striped red and white—were favorites in England, used by cooks in a wide assortment of sweet and savory dishes. During the Regency, naughty and nice ladies used the beet juice to seductively stain their lips and redden their cheeks. Beets have long been associated with amorous desire; the goddess of love, Aphrodite, is said to have consumed beet juice in preparation for her passionate trysts.

Fish

———◆———

The Port of London is truly a magical place, as ships arrive from across the colonies, bringing with them all forms of new and exciting foods and spices (and perhaps a few unruly stowaways). Barnacled hulls waltz upon the waves, and the docks are packed with sailors and merchants ready to take the fresh bounty to market. And most notably, heaps of fresh fish of all shapes and colors blanket the horizon, ready to make their way to the kitchens of the ton. And what is more suitable a dish to an island nation than fish? Every feast was sure to offer glorious platters of cod and salmon and other tasty offerings from the surrounding seas. Though without government oversight, our Regency shoppers had to have a savvy nose to sniff out potentially poor-quality wares.

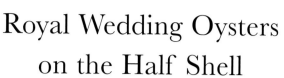

Royal Wedding Oysters
on the Half Shell

*While the scoundrels engage in salacious and sacrilegious practices,
weddings are a place of virtue and true love. It is a time for all to celebrate and
rejoice the unions of the intendeds with grace. And what more graceful a food
than the oyster to celebrate such a union? It represents purity and fertility,
and its marriage with these two sauces is truly a blessing.*

MAKES 24 OYSTERS

For Oysters
2 medium lemons, halved
2 dozen fresh oysters on half shell
4 cups crushed ice

For Mignonette Sauce
$1/2$ cup high-quality white balsamic vinegar
$1/4$ cup finely diced shallot
1 teaspoon granulated sugar
$1/2$ teaspoon salt
$1/4$ teaspoon ground white pepper

For Chimichurri Sauce
$1/2$ cup cold-pressed olive oil
$1/4$ medium red bell pepper, seeded and finely diced
$1/4$ medium red onion, peeled and finely diced
$1/4$ red Fresno chile, finely diced
1 clove garlic, peeled and finely diced
$1/2$ teaspoon salt
$1/2$ teaspoon ground black pepper
2 tablespoons finely chopped fresh parsley

CONTINUED

CONTINUED

1. To make Oysters: Squeeze lemons over oysters. Place oysters on a large serving dish over crushed ice.

2. To make Mignonette Sauce: Mix all ingredients in a small bowl until sugar has dissolved. Set aside.

3. To make Chimichurri Sauce: Mix all ingredients together in a small bowl and let sit up to 12 hours for flavors to combine. Serve Sauces alongside Oysters for dipping.

. . . .

WEDDINGS

Weddings during the Regency were generally not ostentatious but small family affairs. They took place before noon, and the groom had to be at least fourteen years old and the bride twelve.

Benedict's Perfected
Cod à la Hollandaise

This is a commingling of contrasts, with the lean, flaky cod melting away within the warmth of the hollandaise sauce. It appeals to lords and ladies of all ages.

SERVES 4

$1/2$ cup plus 2 tablespoons melted unsalted butter, divided

2 large sprigs fresh tarragon, divided

3 large egg yolks, pasteurized

1 teaspoon white vinegar

1 tablespoon fresh lemon juice

$1/2$ teaspoon kosher salt

2 tablespoons unsalted butter

1 teaspoon sea salt

$1/8$ teaspoon ground white pepper (optional)

1 pound cod fillet, quartered

1. In a small saucepan over low heat, add $1/2$ cup butter and 1 sprig tarragon and gently melt butter. Allow tarragon to gently simmer 3 minutes, then remove from heat. Remove tarragon from pan.

2. In a blender, mix egg yolks, vinegar, lemon juice, and kosher salt until creamy. With blender on low speed, slowly mix in melted butter. Set aside.

3. Sprinkle sea salt and white pepper on cod pieces. In a medium pan over medium-high heat, add remaining 2 tablespoons butter and cod. Cook cod 3 minutes on each side until flaky through center and internal temperature reaches 145°F.

4. Place cod on a large plate and cover with sauce. Garnish with leaves from remaining sprig tarragon.

. . . . . .

COD

Cod during the Regency was considered not just delicious but a national treasure. Eighteenth-century statesman William Pitt the Elder called it "British gold." It proved a valuable staple for sailors and explorers.

Colonial Scallops with Lime and Cilantro Aioli

A banquet at Queen Charlotte and King George's would likely have included a luxurious dish such as this. Not only is it daringly sophisticated, but it is also extremely easy on the eyes. For those cooking at their private estates, this dish can be ready in a few hours and takes but a few moments to prepare.

SERVES 6

For Cilantro Aioli
¹⁄₂ cup chopped fresh cilantro
2 medium cloves garlic, peeled
¹⁄₃ cup olive oil
1 large egg yolk, pasteurized
¹⁄₂ teaspoon sea salt

For Scallops
3 large limes
6 large scallops
6 teaspoons extra-virgin olive oil
6 teaspoons Cilantro Aioli (see recipe)
1 medium jalapeño, chopped and seeded
1 bunch fresh cilantro
¹⁄₄ small red onion, peeled and thinly sliced

1. To Make Cilantro Aioli: Add cilantro and garlic to a blender. Turn blender to high speed and slowly add oil. Add egg yolk and salt. Blend until smooth. Pour into a small sealable container and store in refrigerator for up to 1 week.

2. To make Scallops: Squeeze juice from limes into a medium glass or plastic bowl. Add scallops, cover, and refrigerate 3 hours up to overnight.

3. Slice marinated scallops thin, about five slices per scallop. To six small plates, add 1 teaspoon oil and then place 1 scallop, with its slices overlapping or side by side, onto oil. Add 1 tablespoon Cilantro Aioli lengthwise along center of each serving. Top with even amounts jalapeño (or to taste). Garnish with cilantro and red onion.

COSTUME DESIGN

Emmy-winning costume designer Ellen Mirojnick headed up the team of over two hundred people in the creation of more than seven thousand five hundred unique costume pieces for the show. In the end there were nearly five thousand outfits. Phoebe Dynevor (Daphne Bridgerton) wore over one hundred of them herself!

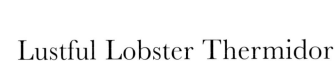

Lustful Lobster Thermidor

*Will the foundation of class and social standing be enough to bear
the crushing weight of scrutiny for our dear ton, whose slightest misdeeds leave
cracks for all to see? It must be mentioned here that Lustful Lobster Thermidor
is perhaps the one dish most impervious to lashing criticism, thanks to its creamy
lobster flavor, beautiful presentation, and ease of preparation.*

SERVES 4

2 whole fresh lobsters

4 tablespoons unsalted butter

$\frac{1}{2}$ medium leek, diced (whites and light greens only)

2 medium cloves garlic, peeled and minced

$\frac{1}{8}$ teaspoon ground mace

$\frac{1}{2}$ teaspoon cayenne pepper

2 tablespoons all-purpose flour

$\frac{1}{2}$ cup whole milk

1 medium lemon, quartered

1 tablespoon salt

$\frac{1}{3}$ cup grated Parmesan or gruyere cheese

$\frac{1}{2}$ cup fresh tarragon or chives

1. Place lobsters in a large pot of boiling water and cook 8–10 minutes until bright red. Remove from water and set aside.

2. In a small saucepan over medium heat, melt butter. Add leek and garlic and cook until soft and translucent, about 5 minutes. Add mace and cayenne pepper.

3. Whisk in flour and cook 2 minutes, then slowly add milk, while whisking, until mixture thickens. Remove from heat and set aside.

CONTINUED

CONTINUED

4. With kitchen shears or a sharp knife, cut lobsters in half lengthwise. Remove claws and legs and clean out innards. Remove meat from tails and claws and cut into ¼" cubes.

5. To each lobster half, add chopped lobster meat, juice from ¼ lemon, and salt. Spoon leek mixture over meat and cover with cheese.

6. Preheat broiler to high. Place lobsters on an ungreased baking sheet and broil on high heat about 3 minutes until tops are golden. Garnish with tarragon or chives and serve immediately.

LOBSTERS

Lobsters were relatively affordable during the Regency era due to their massive population. Shoppers at the markets would have to be well versed in sniffing out old and spoiled foods, as there was no government oversight on quality control.

Gregory's Favorite Terrine

Even though everyone dressed up for dinner and ate the most delectable
of dishes (such as this one), some things never change. Young Hyacinth and Gregory
still manage to fight at the table and fling their peas! A good terrine
is quite a proper dish for both formal and informal dinners.

SERVES 8

1$\frac{1}{2}$ **pounds boneless, skinless salmon fillet**
2 teaspoons paprika
6 tablespoons heavy cream, divided
1 teaspoon sea salt
1 teaspoon ground black pepper
1 cup cooked peas
$\frac{1}{2}$ **cup fresh parsley**
9 large eggs

1. Preheat oven to 350°F.

2. In a food processor, blend salmon, paprika, 3 tablespoons cream, salt, and pepper. Grease terrine with unsalted butter. Spread with 2"–2$\frac{1}{2}$" salmon blend.

3. Clean out processor. Add peas and blend. Add parsley, remaining 3 tablespoons cream, and eggs, and blend until smooth.

4. Spread pea mixture over salmon in terrine. Layer remaining salmon blend on top of pea layer. Cover terrine and place in a hot water bath in oven 1 hour.

5. Refrigerate until ready to serve, up to 5 days. To serve, uncover and slice.

TERRINES

Although they epitomize the height of elegance and good taste, terrines are not hard to make. *Terrine* refers to almost anything cooked in a mold or container. Originated by French cooks, the terrine mold is usually made of pottery or earthenware and provides an easy and graceful way to cook meats and game, although fish and vegetable terrines are increasingly popular among the younger members of the ton.

Dueling Swordfish Skewers
with Pesto

*Fresh swordfish is simply divine, and when served on skewers,
it makes lovely finger food to accompany drinks or a fabulous main meal.
But keep those skewers away from the children! One doesn't want them
poking the ladies sitting next to them!*

SERVES 4

For Pesto
1 bunch (about 1½ cups) fresh basil or cilantro
2 medium cloves garlic, peeled
¼ cup Parmesan cheese
⅓ cup pine nuts
⅓ cup extra-virgin olive oil
¼ teaspoon salt

For Swordfish Skewers
1 pound swordfish, cut into bite-sized pieces
1 teaspoon canola (or other neutral) oil
1 teaspoon sea salt
1 teaspoon ground black pepper

1. To make Pesto: Blend all ingredients in a food processor until smooth. Add another clove garlic and blend again if desired. Set aside.

2. To make Swordfish Skewers: Preheat grill to medium-high heat. Soak 4 thin wooden skewers in a large bowl of water 20 minutes.

3. Thread fish onto skewers (four to five pieces per skewer). Brush fish with oil and sprinkle on salt and pepper.

4. Grill skewers 10 minutes, turning every few minutes to evenly cook each side. Fish is cooked when internal temperature reaches 145°F.

5. Transfer Swordfish Skewers to a clean large plate. Add a little Pesto along the length of each skewer and serve the rest in a small bowl on the side for dipping.

· · · · · · · · ·

PESTO

The word *pesto* comes from the Italian word meaning "to pound or crush"— and is made by pounding garlic, herbs, pine nuts, and cheese (usually Parmesan or another hard, aged cheese) with a pestle. Mediterranean cultures have versions of this dish dating back to ancient Roman times. While basil is the most widely used herb in pesto, Daphne loves cilantro and insists her cook use that in her pesto.

Lady Bridgerton's Salmon Tartare

When you simply must have the finest spread for esteemed guests,
this dish is sure to crease any dandy's cravat. Its luxurious texture and playful
ginger notes will awaken even the most plebeian of palates. Pay your fishmonger
a few shillings extra for the freshest salmon and serve on chips or crackers.
Garnish with extra dill and lime slices.

SERVES 4

½ pound sushi-grade salmon
½ cup fresh dill
Juice of 1 small lime
1 medium shallot, peeled and diced
1 tablespoon fresh grated ginger
2 teaspoons extra-virgin olive oil
½ teaspoon salt

Add all ingredients to a food processor. Pulse until ingredients are minced but not puréed.

TARTARE

Tartare cries out for the finest ingredients. For the best olive oil,
look for the extra-virgin designation, cold-pressed extraction of recently harvested
olives (no additives or chemicals). This is a food so delicious that it can
be savored by itself without cooking.

Brimsley's Baked Salmon

*Salmon, the royalty of the fish family, was a great favorite of the Britons,
as much of it came from Scotland and Ireland. Salmon can be prepared in a
myriad of ways, but this baked salmon is easy to prepare and worthy of a visit
from Queen Charlotte herself! Brimsley orders the kitchen staff to prepare this to
lighten the queen's mood every time a society paper is published.*

SERVES 12

For Basil Garlic Sauce
$1/2$ **cup fresh basil leaves**
2 medium cloves garlic, peeled
$4^{1}/2$ **tablespoons high-quality extra-virgin olive oil**
$1/2$ **teaspoon sea salt**
$1/4$ **teaspoon whole red peppercorns**

For Salmon
1 (3-pound) boneless, skinless salmon fillet
2 large heirloom tomatoes, sliced
$1/4$ **cup Basil Garlic Sauce (see recipe)**

1. To make Basil Garlic Sauce: In a food processor, blend basil, garlic, and oil.
   Add salt and peppercorns and pulse once.

2. To make Salmon: Preheat oven to 400°F. Grease a large ceramic or glass
   baking dish with olive oil.

3. Place salmon in dish. Place tomato slices along length of salmon. Top with Basil Garlic Sauce.

4. Bake 20 minutes uncovered until fish reaches an internal temperature of 145°F. Serve from baking dish or place Salmon on a large platter.

BASIL GARLIC SAUCE

The Basil Garlic Sauce in this recipe is a variation of pesto, although much lighter. The quality of the olive oil defines this sauce. If you do not have the very best olive oil, add a pasteurized raw egg yolk during the final pulse of the food processor. Pesto also works well with this dish. Rumors have it that the Bridgerton cook would at times bake the salmon with pesto on top, and that was a hit with the ton as well!

Meats

For curing an insatiable appetite for all things lascivious in nature, meats are by far the most filling and satisfying. Whole game and roasts are the center of any dinner, and their presentation summons the carnal spirits much as Caravaggio does with oils. Meats make up the majority of dishes of a Regency feast, and their presence and nature speak highly of the host. Don't let the sight of whole animals displayed upon the table shake you, dear reader, for it is a source of pride for the lords who hunt on their estates to present the fruits of their pastimes like consumable gemstones from the family coffers. Whole roasts, game birds, and refined dishes should enamor and excite the senses, their sustenance serving the propensity of entitled man. The only thing one may have a greater appetite for than meat is seeing one's enemy skewered by a sharp spear of accusation.

Regency Pie

This pie is as renowned for its good looks as it is for its flaky crust and deliciously sweet, meaty filling. Its place is in the center of the table so all guests may equally gaze upon its splendor.

SERVES 8

For Crust
3 cups all-purpose flour
³⁄₄ teaspoon kosher salt
1 teaspoon baking powder
3 tablespoons light brown sugar
¹⁄₃ cup vegetable shortening
¹⁄₃ cup cold unsalted butter, cut in ¹⁄₄" cubes
1¹⁄₄ cups buttermilk

For Filling
3 tablespoons vegetable oil
1 medium yellow onion, peeled and diced
4 cups chopped white button mushrooms
4 medium cloves garlic, peeled
1¹⁄₂ teaspoons kosher salt
3 cups ground beef, pork, or chicken (or a combination)
5 teaspoons barbecue sauce
1¹⁄₂ cups beef broth
3 tablespoons cornstarch

1. To make Crust: In a food processor, pulse flour, salt, baking powder, and sugar. Add shortening and butter and pulse until butter pieces are pea-sized or smaller.

2. Move dough to a large bowl and slowly mix in buttermilk until sticky. Wrap in plastic wrap and refrigerate until ready to use.

CONTINUED

3. To make Filling: In a large saucepan over medium heat, add oil and onion and cook until translucent, about 10 minutes. Add mushrooms and cook 10 minutes, stirring often.

4. Add garlic, salt, and meat and cook until meat is fully cooked, about 15 minutes. Add barbecue sauce and broth and let simmer 5 minutes, then add cornstarch and mix well until thickened. Add more cornstarch if needed. Filling should be thick enough that if you scrape bottom of pan with a spatula, filling won't fill in.

5. Remove pan from heat and transfer to a medium heat-safe bowl. chill 1 hour.

6. To assemble: Preheat oven to 400°F. Grease an 8" springform pan with nonstick cooking spray.

7. Remove dough from refrigerator and roll ⅔ out into a 12" circle about ¼" thick. Lay dough over pan. Carefully press dough into pan, making sure there are no holes.

8. Add Filling to pan, leaving 1"–2" at top of pan. Roll out remaining dough and cover and seal over Filling. Poke several small holes in top of dough and bake 30 minutes.

9. Remove from oven and let rest in pan 15 minutes. Transfer pie out of pan onto a large plate. Slice and serve.

STANDING PIES

Standing pies are so named because they are able to stand up on their own without the use of a pie dish. This is due to the very thick crust. Though often served hot, savory standing pies allow the meat within to last for weeks, as the juices can be drained out and replaced with butter or fat to eliminate air contact. It was rumored that while King George was ill, he was served a treat of a standing pie filled with live birds that flew out upon cutting the crust!

Oxford Roasted Beef Heart
with Lemon Confit

*Sometimes, as luck would have it, you may find yourself seated next to
an unpleasant guest at the night's soiree. It's difficult enough to have to make small talk.
But to do so while eating is most cruel indeed. Roasted beef heart is so flavorful and
nutritious it will surely make the room go silent until the course is finished.*

SERVES 4

2 medium lemons, cut into ⅛"-thick slices
2 tablespoons granulated sugar
1 tablespoon kosher salt
2 teaspoons sea salt
1 tablespoon very coarse ground black pepper
1 pound beef heart, cut into ¼"-thick slices
3 tablespoons extra-virgin olive oil

1. Place lemon slices in a medium glass jar and mix in sugar and kosher salt. Allow to sit at least 2 weeks in refrigerator.

2. Remove lemon slices from refrigerator and thoroughly rinse. With a mortar and pestle, purée flesh and rinds and set aside.

3. Generously apply sea salt and pepper to beef heart slices. In a large cast iron pan over high heat, heat oil. Add sliced beef heart and sear 1–2 minutes on each side until caramelized and an internal temperature of at least 145°F is reached.

4. Remove from heat and allow to rest 10 minutes in the pan. Use a pastry brush to paint on lemon confit and serve immediately.

NOSE-TO-TAIL BUTCHERY

Nose-to-tail butchery was the standard, not the exception, during the Regency. All parts of the animal were used in one way or another. Offal, or organ meats, was considered a delicacy and is still a common dish to this day.

Lady Varley's Spicy Chicken

Some have the misfortune of falling from grace due to no fault of their own, while others, it would appear, gladly embark on the dark road of depravity. Lady Varley's is one such soul. In this roasted chicken recipe, ginger, paprika, and cinnamon share quite the passion for each other. And served with Sweet Tomato Jam, this dish is an enticing spectacle indeed. Though traditionally cooked as a whole chicken, this recipe works splendidly with boneless, skinless thighs.

SERVES 8

For Sweet Tomato Jam
2 tablespoons canola (or other neutral) oil
1 medium clove garlic, peeled and minced
2 cups canned diced tomatoes, including 3 teaspoons liquid
2 tablespoons dark brown sugar
$\frac{1}{4}$ teaspoon ground cumin
1 tablespoon fresh grated ginger

For Spicy Chicken
$\frac{1}{2}$ tablespoon kosher salt
$\frac{1}{2}$ tablespoon ground black pepper
$\frac{1}{2}$ tablespoon paprika
$\frac{1}{2}$ teaspoon ground cinnamon
$\frac{1}{2}$ teaspoon ground ginger
8 (4-ounce) boneless, skinless chicken breasts,
each breast cut into eight thin slices
4 tablespoons extra-virgin olive oil
2 cups Sweet Tomato Jam (see recipe)
1 small bunch fresh cilantro, chopped

1. To make Sweet Tomato Jam: In a medium saucepan over medium heat, add oil and garlic. Once garlic becomes fragrant, about 3 minutes, add tomatoes, reserved liquid, sugar, and cumin. Cook 5 minutes until sauce thickens. Add ginger, mix, and remove from heat.

2. To make Spicy Chicken: In a small bowl, mix salt, pepper, paprika, cinnamon, and ginger well, making sure there are no clumps. Cover chicken generously with rub.

3. In a large cast iron or heavy-bottomed skillet over high heat, add oil. Once oil is hot, add chicken and cook 4 minutes per side until chicken is thoroughly cooked and golden brown. Internal temperature should be at least 165°F.

4. Serve chicken topped with Sweet Tomato Jam and cilantro.

. . . .

SPICES

In the early nineteenth century, spices from around the world were making their way into English households—especially the wealthy ones. Spices were widely circulated, and increasingly understood to be necessary for the good, and flavorful, life. It would not be uncommon to find paprika, curry, cardamom, ginger, nutmeg, and others made available through the spice trade.

Pineapple Centerpiece
with Pork Belly

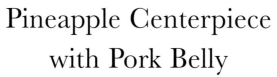

*A specialty from the staff at the Duke of Hastings's palace, pork belly
from the local pig farmers is transformed into small, spicy bites and served in
a pineapple. It's a pairing as enchanting as any in Bridgerton.*

SERVES 4

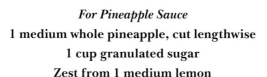

For Pineapple Sauce
1 medium whole pineapple, cut lengthwise
1 cup granulated sugar
Zest from 1 medium lemon

For Pork
1 teaspoon paprika
1 teaspoon ground cumin
1 tablespoon sea salt
1 teaspoon ground black pepper
1 pound pork belly, cut into 1" cubes
¼ cup vegetable oil
2 tablespoons chopped fresh cilantro or watercress

1. To make Pineapple Sauce: Scoop out pineapple halves, saving pineapple "shells." Cut pineapple into ½" cubes. Place 1 cup pineapple cubes in a blender and pulse until they turn to liquid. Set remaining pineapple cubes aside.

2. Add pineapple juice to a small saucepan with sugar and stir over low heat until sugar is dissolved, about 5 minutes.

3. Add lemon zest and continue stirring 2 minutes, then set aside to cool and thicken while cooking Pork.

CONTINUED

4. To make Pork: Preheat oven to 275°F.

5. In a small bowl, mix paprika, cumin, salt, and pepper. Gently coat each of Pork cubes in paprika mix and set aside.

6. In a large cast iron pan, add oil to just coat bottom and bring to 400°F over high heat. Gently add Pork and sear on each side, cooking 2 minutes total. Remove from heat and add to an ungreased large baking dish.

7. Add Pineapple Sauce and cover Pork with aluminum foil. Bake 45 minutes until pork is very tender and internal temperature is at least 165°F.

8. Mix pork and remaining pineapple cubes and serve inside pineapple "shells." Garnish with cilantro or watercress.

PINEAPPLES

Pineapples were extremely rare during the Regency era and were often used at balls and other banquets as table decoration, normally in the form of old and rotten specimens. Those with great wealth might have had a pinery on their estate, which was essentially a large greenhouse devoted to growing pineapples.

Citrus-Glazed Quails à la Hastings

When a gentleman visits the country, hunting is one of his favorite pastimes. Game birds have a deeper flavor than chicken and are complemented well with bright, zesty flavors. Recipes like this would have been a favorite of the Duke of Hastings and would likely be prepared by Mrs. Colson's most revered chef.

SERVES 4

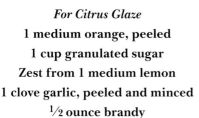

For Citrus Glaze	*For Quails*
1 medium orange, peeled	4 (4-ounce) quails
1 cup granulated sugar	2 tablespoons extra-virgin olive oil
Zest from 1 medium lemon	1 teaspoon sea salt
1 clove garlic, peeled and minced	¼ cup Citrus Glaze (see recipe)
½ ounce brandy	4 sprigs fresh rosemary

1. To make Citrus Glaze: In a food processor, blend orange and sugar.

2. Pour into a small saucepan over low heat and stir constantly 3 minutes until sugar has dissolved. Add lemon zest and garlic. Continue to stir 1 minute. Add brandy and cook down, another 3 minutes.

3. Remove from heat and allow to cool, about 5 minutes.

4. To make Quails: Preheat oven to 400°F.

5. Lightly brush Quails with oil and cover with sea salt. Bake 30 minutes in a large greased baking dish or on a grill.

6. Remove from oven or grill and test for doneness. Internal temperature should be at least 165°F. Brush generously on all sides with Citrus Glaze. Place back in oven and bake 5 minutes until glaze sets. Remove from oven and allow to cool 10 minutes before serving.

7. Serve on large plates, garnished with rosemary.

GLAZING

Glazing sweet and savory dishes has been very popular in England since medieval times. Just add sugar to orange juice, water, or egg whites and brush onto just about anything. Too much is never enough!

The Gambler's Duck

*Any banquet worthy of mention would surely have a roast duck or two,
always with the perfect glaze to glisten in the candlelight. The important thing to
remember when cooking duck breast is that you must cook it skin-side down and bring
the heat up slowly so that the fats in the skin can gradually get hot and render,
making them crispy. Adorn this dish with cherry Compote and Curd for some
nice colors, and pair it with the night's Bordeaux.*

SERVES 4

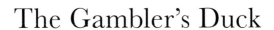

For Curd
4 cups whole milk
$\frac{1}{2}$ teaspoon curd culture

For Compote
2 cups pitted cherries
$1\frac{1}{2}$ cups water
$\frac{1}{2}$ cup granulated sugar
3 tablespoons dry red wine
$\frac{1}{2}$ teaspoon herbes de Provence
$\frac{1}{8}$ teaspoon ground allspice
1 tablespoon unsalted butter
1 teaspoon lemon juice

For Duck
1 (4-pound) duck, innards removed, refrigerated overnight uncovered

1. To make Curd: In a small pan over medium-high heat, slowly bring milk
   to a boil. Once boiling, remove from heat and let cool to lukewarm, about
   15 minutes.

2. Add curd culture and mix well. Cover and keep in a warm place 8 hours
   to set.

CONTINUED

3. To make Compote: In a small saucepan over medium heat, add cherries, water, and sugar. Cook 20 minutes, stirring often, until cherries break down and sugar dissolves. When mixture begins to thicken, spoon out 2 tablespoons liquid and set aside in a small bowl.

4. Increase heat to medium-high and add wine, herbes de Provence, and allspice. Cook until wine cooks away and mixture is thick, about 10 minutes. Remove from heat and add butter and lemon juice. Set aside.

5. To make Duck: Preheat oven to 275°F. With the duck breast-side up, carefully score skin without cutting down meat. Place Duck breast-side up in a large baking dish. Bake 1 hour. After 1 hour, prick skin again and flip Duck. Bake another 1 hour.

6. Increase oven temperature to 325°F. Flip Duck breast-side up and bake 1 more hour. After 1 hour, baste Duck all over with reserved cherry liquid. Increase oven temperature to 425°F and bake Duck 10–15 minutes until cherry liquid has caramelized, keeping an eye on skin so it doesn't burn.

7. Remove from oven and allow to rest 15 minutes uncovered before serving alongside Curd and Compote for topping.

HUNTING

For the upper class, hunting was done mainly for sport, and lords would often have several horses just for this pastime so they could hunt daily. Hunting, however, also provided the fresh meat and game for mealtimes, so the ladies of the house had no grounds for complaint!

King George's Roast Lamb with Tarragon and Mango Relish

Poor King George III's priceless crown sits ever so precariously on a man confined by madness behind the opulent walls of Buckingham Palace. Still, one might well go mad over this timeless roast, for its harmony and grace know no bounds. Any table adorned by this dish requires nothing more to be a royal feast.

SERVES 6

For Lamb
2 racks grass-fed lamb with 7 bones each, excess fat removed
3 tablespoons olive oil
4 tablespoons sea salt
4 tablespoons ground black pepper
3 sprigs fresh tarragon

For Relish
1 cup fresh mango cubes
$\frac{1}{2}$ large green bell pepper, seeded
$\frac{1}{2}$ small Vidalia or sweet onion, peeled
$\frac{3}{4}$ cup fresh cilantro or parsley
1 tablespoon fresh grated ginger
1 tablespoon amber honey
$\frac{1}{4}$ cup pulp-free orange juice
1 teaspoon fresh lemon juice (optional)
$\frac{1}{2}$ small, seeded jalapeño (optional)

1. To make Lamb: Preheat oven to 450°F.

2. Gently coat ribs with oil, salt, and pepper. In a large oven-safe pan over medium-high heat, gently sear back side (fat side) of ribs 5 minutes.

3. Place pan on middle rack in oven and bake 12 minutes until internal temperature reaches 145°F. Remove pan and set aside.

4. To make Relish: Add all ingredients to a food processor. Pulse until finely chopped. Slice lamb between the bones and spoon on Relish. Garnish with fresh tarragon and serve.

. . . .

MAD KING GEORGE

King George III became incapacitated with mental illness, and in 1811 his son George became the prince regent. Much of his mental collapse was attributed to the death of his fifteenth daughter, Princess Amelia.

Clyvedon's Best Shoulder of Pork

Noble and forgiving, the pork shoulder never falls from grace.
Set it on a platter with Sweet Tomato Jam or combine with spices for a savory
pie. If your lord fancies his meat smoked, perhaps call one of the kitchen staff to
smoke it in the hearth. Once cooked, pull the pork and use it as an
alternative filling for Clyvedon Market Pies (see recipe in this chapter), or
serve alongside the night's other fare.

SERVES 10

For Heritage Brine
1 gallon water
1 cup dark brown sugar
1 cup kosher salt
1 cup dried seaweed
1 cup dried shiitake mushrooms
2 tablespoons blue cheese

For Pork
1 (8-pound) pork shoulder, skin removed
Sweet Tomato Jam

1. To make Heritage Brine: In a large pot over high heat, bring water to a boil. Add sugar, salt, seaweed, and mushrooms and reduce heat to low. Simmer 5 minutes. Add blue cheese and stir until dissolved.

2. Remove from heat and let cool, about 1 hour. Once cool, refrigerate until cold, about 2 hours.

3. To make Pork: In a large sealable plastic bag or container, add Pork and Heritage Brine. Meat should be totally submerged. Refrigerate 3 days.

4. Preheat oven to 275°F.

5. Remove Pork from Heritage Brine and rinse in cold water to remove any seaweed. Pat dry and place in a large baking dish greased with oil or unsalted butter. Bake 6 hours.

6. With a pastry brush, generously spread Sweet Tomato Jam over Pork and wrap in foil, making sure to completely cover all sides. Increase oven to 325°F and bake 3 hours. Remove foil and bake an additional 30 minutes until Pork reaches an internal temperature of at least 145°F.

. . . .

PIG'S HEAD

Almost the quintessential image of an outlandish and carnal feast, the pig's head served on a platter was of course very popular during the Regency. The tongue was considered a delicacy. Wild boar was also highly prized. The men would do the slicing and serve the ladies next to them.

Winning Pig Bacon Bites

These small, four-bite pies are golden and flaky on the outside and warm and sweet on the inside. One can be sure they came from the fair's winning pig.

MAKES 6 PIES

For Crust
2 cups all-purpose flour
$1/2$ teaspoon kosher salt
$3/4$ teaspoon baking powder
2 tablespoons light brown sugar
$1/4$ cup vegetable shortening
$1/4$ cup cold unsalted butter, cut in $1/4$" cubes
$3/4$ cup buttermilk

For Filling
1 pound bacon strips, cut into $1/4$" pieces
$1/4$ teaspoon sea salt
6 tablespoons pure maple syrup

1. To make Crust: Add flour, kosher salt, baking powder, and sugar to a food processor. Pulse to mix. Add shortening and butter; pulse until butter is pea-sized.

2. Transfer mixture into a large bowl and slowly add buttermilk until a wet dough forms. Separate dough into six even balls. On a clean, lightly floured surface, roll out each ball into a 5" circle $1/4$" thick and set aside.

3. To make Filling: Preheat oven to 400°F.

4. In a large pan over medium heat, cook bacon until fat renders, about 15 minutes. Discard fat or save for later use. Place bacon in a medium bowl and add sea salt and maple syrup. Refrigerate 15 minutes until mixture thickens.

5. Add 1 large spoonful bacon to center of each Crust and then pull up edges of dough and squeeze together at top. Make sure there are no holes.

6. Grease a large baking sheet with nonstick cooking spray. Flip pies over and space 2" apart on baking sheet. Bake 25–30 minutes until golden brown. Serve warm.

. . . .

FARMING

During the Regency era, the majority of the population lived in the countryside and farmed for a living. The introduction of crop rotation in the 1800s allowed for the production of more produce and livestock, contributing to the agricultural revolution.

Clyvedon Market Pies

*Fully enclosed pies like the ones sold at the market outside Clyvedon
Castle are stout and can be filled with just about anything one cares for—from
smoked beef brisket or pork butt to seasonal vegetables or curries. Consider using
stamps or molds to decorate your pies. Please note that this recipe requires
the use of glass Mason jars to form the molds for the pie crusts, so sizes
may vary. This recipe calls for two pint-sized jars.*

MAKES 2 PIES

For Crusts
2 cups bread flour
1 teaspoon salt
5 tablespoons unsalted butter, softened
$^1\!/_2$ cup water
1 large egg, beaten

For Filling
2 pounds grass-fed ground beef
8 slices bacon, diced small
1 medium red onion, peeled and diced
$^1\!/_2$ cup golden raisins
$^1\!/_2$ cup chopped dill pickles
$1^1\!/_2$ cups water
1 (0.25-ounce) packet unflavored gelatin
$1^1\!/_2$ cups barbecue sauce

1. To make Crust: In a large bowl, combine flour and salt. With your hands, mix in butter, then add water slowly while continuing to mix until a dough forms.

2. Separate dough into two equal balls. From each ball, remove a chunk about the size of a golf ball. On a clean, lightly floured surface, roll out remaining dough into two $^1\!/_4$"-thick circles about 10" in diameter. Wrap outside of a pint-sized Mason jar in plastic wrap and place one jar in center of each dough circle. Carefully form dough around outside of jar, making sure thickness is even and there are no holes.

3. Roll out smaller dough pieces to create two pie tops. Make a hole ¾" in diameter in center of each top and refrigerate on a separate plate along with dough-covered jars 30 minutes.

4. Preheat oven to 300°F. Grease a baking sheet with oil or unsalted butter.

5. Remove dough from refrigerator and carefully separate from jars and plastic wrap. If this is difficult, try filling jars with hot water to soften dough a bit. Set Crust bottoms and tops aside.

6. To make Filling: In a large skillet, combine beef, bacon, and onions. Cook over medium-high heat 10–12 minutes until meats are fully cooked and reach an internal temperature of 145°F. Mix in raisins and pickles and transfer mixture to a large bowl. Allow to cool 30 minutes before covering and refrigerating 1 hour.

7. In a small saucepan over low heat, add water and gelatin. Stir until gelatin has dissolved, about 5 minutes. Remove from heat and stir in barbecue sauce. Allow mixture to cool to room temperature, about 5 minutes, then mix in meat.

8. Fill Crust bottoms with meat mixture. Add Crust tops, pinching around edges to seal. Brush tops with egg and place on prepared baking sheet. Bake 45 minutes.

9. Remove from oven and allow to cool 30 minutes before serving.

· · · · · · · · · · ·

CRUSTS

Originally, crusts were added to pies in order to help preserve the meats within them; they weren't intended to be eaten. This was to make the meats suitable for traveling, whether to one's country estate or on a sea journey.

CHAPTER 5

Evening Sweets and Libations

As the streets of Grosvenor Square fall dark and members of the ton retreat behind closed doors, only intrigue and speculation remain, and these, dear reader, are the ingredients for a most unsavory dish. For even the most majestic rose, once removed from the sun, may wither and wilt. What happens behind closed doors must remain hidden, until the morning sun shines redemption.

Though the men of Bridgerton are quite free to drink wherever they please, for the respectable married ladies of the ton, there is Lady Danbury's den of iniquity, where one may lose one's virtue, if only just for the night. Gambling, gossip, and, most of all, tantalizing drinks to fuel the night's activities are the highlights of any menu. They are sure to test one's virtue if one wishes. And at dinner with guests, the evening's desserts are a final, breathtaking, and climactic end to an outrageously excessive production. A final course includes pies, fruits, ice creams, and, of course, more deliciously tempting drinks. So alert the servants and loosen your linens; it's time for the *fin de spectacle*!

The Duke's Favorite Gooseberry Pie

*The Bridgerton ladies surely do know a thing or two about seducing Simon.
First, Lady Bridgerton serves his favorite dessert: gooseberry pie. Then Daphne uses
her interpretation of a painting to woo him into love and marriage. Note: A pie
of such glamour should be decorated accordingly. Consider using a mold—
perhaps of a flower or another design—to decorate the top crust.*

SERVES 8

For Crust
2 cups all-purpose flour
$1/2$ teaspoon kosher salt
3 tablespoons light brown sugar
$1/4$ cup vegetable shortening
$1/4$ cup cold unsalted butter, cut in $1/4$" cubes
$3/4$ cup cold water

For Filling
1 (15-ounce) can gooseberries with syrup
3 tablespoons unsalted butter
2 medium Honeycrisp apples, peeled, cored, and diced
1 cup granulated sugar
1 teaspoon ground cinnamon
2 tablespoons amber honey
1 cup elderflower lemonade

1. To make Crust: In a large bowl, combine flour, salt, and brown sugar. Add
   shortening and butter and work mixture with your hands until it resembles
   coarse sand. Slowly add cold water while mixing until dough forms a ball.
   Separate into two equal balls.

CONTINUED

2. On a clean, lightly floured surface, roll out dough balls into two 2¼"-thick circles. Cover with plastic wrap and refrigerate 1 hour up to overnight.

3. Preheat oven to 400°F.

4. To make Filling: In a medium pot over medium heat, cook gooseberries with syrup, butter, and apples until apples become soft, about 15 minutes.

5. Add granulated sugar, cinnamon, and honey and cook until sugar dissolves, about 10 minutes. Pour in lemonade and cook down until mixture becomes thick, about 5 minutes.

6. Line a 9" springform tart pan with one dough disc. Remove Filling from heat and allow to cool 30 minutes before pouring into pan. With the second disc of dough, carefully cover pie and pinch edges between your thumb and fingers to seal. Cut five slits in top Crust. Bake 20 minutes or until Crust becomes golden brown. Remove from oven and cool 30 minutes before serving.

GOOSEBERRIES

Gooseberries were used in everything during the Regency. They would be eaten raw as a refreshing snack, used to complement the evening's meats, or made into pastries. Yellow gooseberries were also used to make wine, which was considered to be better than champagne—another way to one-up the French!

Rose of the First Water Pudding

Guests will be left speechless with this creative take on pudding.
It's a beautiful dish made to be adorned with all kinds of fruits and spices.
Garnish with chopped or ground pistachios, shredded coconut,
passion fruit, or pomegranate arils.

SERVES 6

6 tablespoons cornstarch
2 cups whole or 2% milk, divided
$\frac{1}{2}$ tablespoon rose water
$\frac{1}{2}$ cup whipping cream
$\frac{1}{4}$ cup granulated sugar

1. In a medium bowl, whisk cornstarch, $\frac{1}{2}$ cup milk, and rose water until dissolved. Set aside.

2. In a small pot over medium-low heat, combine remaining $1\frac{1}{2}$ cups milk, whipping cream, and sugar and bring to a simmer. Once simmering, add cornstarch mixture and stir constantly until it thickens, about 2 minutes. (Don't let it thicken too much, or pudding will become rubbery.)

3. Remove from heat and pour into six small serving dishes. Cover dishes with plastic wrap and bring to room temperature, about 45 minutes, before refrigerating 2 hours or until quite cold, then serve.

ROSE WATER

Rose water was commonly used as a flavoring for icings, custards, creams, and many other sweets during the Regency era. It was also used historically for its medicinal properties to treat inflammation, anxiety, depression, and sleep disorders. It was also used as eye drops to treat many eye maladies.

Mango Curd Tarts Befitting Royalty

*Even guests who have eaten their fill and drunk themselves sleepy
are sure to be aroused for this* fin de spectacle. *These tarts are so sensual and
the mango so tropically sweet, you're sure to arouse even the bleariest of blokes.
Top with Sugared Berries (see recipe in Chapter 1) if you please.*

MAKES 5 TARTS

For Curd
1 medium ripe mango, peeled and diced
1 large egg
1 large egg yolk
⅛ teaspoon salt
¼ cup superfine or granulated sugar
4 tablespoons cold unsalted butter, cut into small chunks

For Tarts
2 large egg yolks
1 teaspoon vanilla extract
⅓ cup raw macadamia nuts
1⅓ cups all-purpose flour
¼ teaspoon salt
⅔ cup confectioners' sugar
8 tablespoons very cold unsalted butter

1. To make Curd: Blend mangoes until very smooth, scraping down the sides
   of the blender often. Work through a fine mesh sieve using a spatula to yield
   about ½ cup.

2. In a small bowl, whisk together egg and egg yolk and add salt. Mix to
   incorporate salt. Add to a 2-quart heavy-bottomed saucepan over low heat.
   Add mango and gently warm 2 minutes.

3. Pour granulated sugar into pan in a slow stream, stirring constantly. Add
   butter, chunk by chunk, stirring after each chunk until completely combined

before adding more. Continue to stir over low heat 3–5 minutes until Curd thickens and coats a spoon well.

4. Remove from heat and transfer to a medium glass container. Cover with plastic wrap, pressing wrap down onto surface of Curd to prevent a skin from forming. Refrigerate 3 hours up to overnight.

5. To make Tarts: In a small bowl, whisk together egg yolks and vanilla until well combined and set aside.

6. In the bowl of a food processor fitted with an S blade, pulse nuts until they turn into a sandy flour. Add remaining dry ingredients and pulse to combine. Scrape down sides with a spatula, mix up a bit, and then pulse again.

7. Cut butter into nut mixture. Pulse until there are no visible butter chunks and you have a sandy mixture. Add egg yolk mixture and mix until just combined.

8. Turn out dough and knead once or twice, shaping into a thin rectangle, and wrap in plastic wrap. Refrigerate dough until well chilled, about 1 hour.

9. Once cold, roll dough out to ⅛"–¼" thickness on a clean, lightly floured surface. If your molds don't have a nonstick surface, grease with unsalted butter. Cut dough into five circles about ½" larger in diameter than tart molds, and gently lift them into molds, pressing down bottoms and sides firmly. Trim excess dough with a paring knife and poke bottom several times with a fork. Freeze molds 30 minutes.

10. Preheat oven to 320°F. After freezing, transfer molds to a baking sheet and bake until lightly brown on edges, about 14–17 minutes. Let cool completely, about 20 minutes, before gently removing crusts from molds.

11. Fill a piping bag with Curd and pipe into crusts. Serve.

. . . .

MANGOES

Surprisingly, mangoes belong to the cashew family! The wealthiest of the ton would have hothouses where they would grow tropical fruits. Mangoes were also pickled to extend their shelf life.

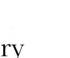

The Royal Flummery

*Majestic and regal in stature, and eliciting high praise upon a
stemmed platter, the flummery (a gelatin dessert) is incomparable: the non plus
ultra of the table. Its appearance declares to the guests they have achieved the highest
level of human dignity and decorum. It is safe to say, dear reader, that the guests were
anything but! This porcelainlike pudding pairs delightfully with Sugared Berries
to make a stunning centerpiece.*

SERVES 16

8 cups whole milk

4 cups heavy cream

3 cups granulated sugar

4 teaspoons vanilla extract

8 tablespoons unflavored gelatin

2 cups Sugared Berries (see recipe in Chapter 1)

3 mint leaves

1. Add all ingredients except Sugared Berries and mint leaves to a large
   saucepan over medium heat. Mix well until sugar and gelatin have dissolved,
   about 15 minutes.

2. Pour mixture into a greased 10" Bundt pan and let cool, about 30 minutes.
   Once cool, cover and refrigerate 4 hours.

3. Turn over onto a large plate and garnish with Sugared Berries and mint
   leaves before serving.

....

FLUMMERY

Flummery was originally made by soaking oatmeal in milk for a savory
dish—quite different from the ornate, sweet dessert that became popular
during the Regency. Oftentimes these gelatinous confections would contain
sweets molded into fish shapes to make the dessert look like an aquarium!

Fervor Sinkers

*After managing the preparations for the ball for hours on end,
one requires a rich and warming drink to be taken by the fire. It's so good to
sip this while relaxing and perhaps writing in one's journal, or tending to
the estate's affairs. This recipe calls for the use of a silicone mold, usually
spherical, but creativity is a virtue. This is a fun drink to make with
the children of the household. Drop in a mug of hot milk and stir for an
impressive cup of cocoa.*

MAKES 8 BALLS

1 (10-ounce) bag milk, white, or dark chocolate chips
3 tablespoons sweetened cocoa powder
$\frac{1}{2}$ cup mini marshmallows
3 tablespoons sprinkles, any color

1. Spray three silicone half-sphere molds (to make eight balls) with nonstick cooking spray. You can work in batches if you have just one or two molds.

2. In a medium microwave-safe bowl, melt chocolate chips on medium in 30-second intervals, stirring well between each cook time until melted. Paint chocolate onto mold using a small pastry brush.

3. Freeze mold 5 minutes or until chocolate is firm. Paint a second coat of chocolate onto mold, taking care to cover entire mold (you may need to remelt chocolate a little). Reserve any leftover chocolate for later use. Freeze 5 more minutes. When solid, use care to remove chocolate from molds.

4. Fill half of molds with cocoa, marshmallows, and sprinkles. Meanwhile, microwave a small microwave-safe plate on high 45 seconds. Run edges of remaining halves of molds along hot plate until they melt slightly. Working quickly, adhere them to filled halves.

5. Place balls on a large plate and freeze 10 minutes until halves are well stuck together.

. . . .

CHOCOLATE

While the history of the cocoa bean goes back three thousand years to ancient Mexico, the powder mixed with sugar became a popular drink in England before the Regency period. When the prince regent reigned, grinding the roasted beans, extracting cocoa and cocoa butter, and mixing with milk and sugar in flourishing chocolate houses was de rigueur for the upper classes. For breakfast, a mid-afternoon or late-afternoon lunch, or a post-opera snack, cocoa was part of the possibilities.

The Innkeeper's Apple Galette

If there had been any time to eat while stopping at the inn on their
wedding night, this would have made for a lovely, rustic dessert for Simon and Daphne.
Serve it with ice cream or Clotted Cream (see recipe in Chapter 2) for added richness.
The dish can be made in any shape and size depending on the number of guests. Add
2 tablespoons of bourbon to the sauce to make this a little more decadent.

SERVES 8

2 tablespoons unsalted butter
2 tablespoons light or dark brown sugar
2$\frac{1}{2}$ heaping cups sliced Gala apples
$\frac{1}{8}$ teaspoon salt
1 sheet puff pastry, thawed but cold to touch
1 teaspoon ground cinnamon
1 large egg, beaten

1. Preheat oven to 400°F. Line a baking sheet with parchment paper.

2. In a medium pan over low heat, melt butter. Add sugar and stir. Add apple slices, sprinkle with salt, and stir often until golden and caramelized, about 10 minutes. Remove from heat.

3. Roll out puff pastry slightly. Transfer to prepared baking sheet. Place apple mixture in middle of puff pastry. Sprinkle with cinnamon and then roughly fold edges of pastry over apples, leaving a large area exposed in the middle.

4. Coat sides of pastry with egg and bake 20–30 minutes until pastry is puffed and golden. Let cool 3 minutes before serving.

. . . .

APPLES

During the Regency, apples were perhaps the most familiar fruit. It would have been common for gentlemen to carry an assortment of tools along with them while out in public to assist ladies who might enjoy an apple for a snack. The tools included a fork to pierce the apple so it could be peeled, a knife for peeling, and often an ornate silver apple corer containing spices in the handle for extra flavor.

Frozen Napoleon

Could there be a finer pleasure than a cooling sweet after a feast?
To cleanse the palate and awaken the spirits, serve this for dessert, especially
on a warm evening. If your palace includes a cold room (freezer), then
beckon a dish hand to whip up this celebratory cake.

SERVES 10

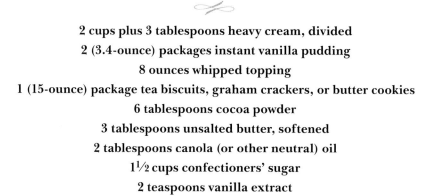

2 cups plus 3 tablespoons heavy cream, divided
2 (3.4-ounce) packages instant vanilla pudding
8 ounces whipped topping
1 (15-ounce) package tea biscuits, graham crackers, or butter cookies
6 tablespoons cocoa powder
3 tablespoons unsalted butter, softened
2 tablespoons canola (or other neutral) oil
1½ cups confectioners' sugar
2 teaspoons vanilla extract

1. Grease a 9" × 13" baking pan with nonstick cooking spray.

2. Combine 2 cups cream and pudding mix in a large bowl. Set aside.

3. In a medium bowl, whip whipped topping 2 minutes until light and fluffy, and fold into pudding mixture.

4. Line bottom of prepared pan with cookies and cover with ½ whipped mixture. Cover with another layer of cookies. Top with remaining whipped mixture. Top whipped layer with remaining cookies.

5. Freeze pan until firm, about 1 hour.

6. Combine cocoa, remaining 3 tablespoons cream, butter, oil, sugar, and vanilla in a medium bowl. Spread over Frozen Napoleon and return to the freezer until firm, about 30 minutes. Serve frozen.

· · · · · · · · · · · · · · · · ·

NAPOLEON

One might be forgiven for thinking that this recipe name refers to the great defeated French ruler and military leader who had recently gone down in ignominy at the Battle of Waterloo. But no! This flaky dream of custard in puff pastry originally came from Naples and was thus called a Napolitan. But let's not allow a few facts to complicate our pleasure; the British still love it!

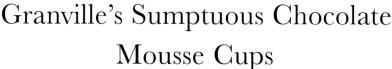

Granville's Sumptuous Chocolate Mousse Cups

So sensual is this dish, it would make even the most licentious of lords blush. And it's quite a breeze to prepare. So if you're planning a Lord Granville–style gathering or something a bit more, well, traditional, make these in advance and enjoy when the appetite is right. Tempt your guests further by garnishing each cup with shaved chocolate and a fresh raspberry.

SERVES 6

4 cups chocolate chips, divided
16 ounces whipped topping
1 large egg, pasteurized

1. Arrange six silicone muffin liners on a baking sheet and lightly spray with nonstick cooking spray.

2. In a small microwave-safe bowl, heat 2 cups chocolate chips on high in 30-second intervals, stirring well between cook times until melted.

3. Using a small pastry brush, generously paint melted chocolate onto bottoms and sides of muffin liners, making sure to fill in any holes and reinforce bottom edges. Refrigerate liners 10 minutes, or freeze 5 minutes, and then apply a second coat of melted chocolate. Refrigerate or freeze again until quite solid.

4. In a medium microwave-safe bowl, microwave remaining 2 cups chocolate chips on medium-high in 30-second intervals, stirring well between cook times until melted.

5. In a separate medium microwave-safe bowl, warm whipped topping in the microwave on high 30 seconds or until warm to the touch.

CONTINUED

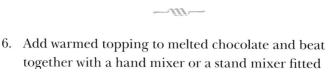

6. Add warmed topping to melted chocolate and beat together with a hand mixer or a stand mixer fitted with a whisk attachment until combined. Let cool for 10 minutes, then add egg and beat until combined.

7. Gently peel solid chocolate cups away from silicone molds and pour in chocolate mixture. Refrigerate 3 hours before serving.

HOMOSEXUALITY

Sir Henry Granville's soirees offer a glimpse into the sexual underground of the Regency. Though homosexuality was a punishable offense, there is much debate about what constituted homosexuality during this time and to whom the penalties might apply. It was common for aristocratic men of the time to partake in all manner of carnal activities, many of which would be considered same-sex in nature by today's standards.

Penelope's Yellow Cake

Poor Penelope is destined for a life in yellow frocks. However, she is much more colorful than any single color, since, as we know, she lives a double life. Hidden behind its ostentatious yellow facade, this cake is tender and loving, like our beloved Penelope. This one-bowl wonder yields a lot of sheet cake, a perfect treat for afternoon guests.

SERVES 12

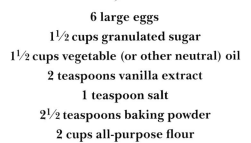

6 large eggs
1½ cups granulated sugar
1½ cups vegetable (or other neutral) oil
2 teaspoons vanilla extract
1 teaspoon salt
2½ teaspoons baking powder
2 cups all-purpose flour

1. Preheat oven to 350°F and grease a 9" × 13" baking dish with nonstick cooking spray.

2. Using a hand mixer, beat eggs in a large bowl until frothy and pale. Add remaining ingredients, one at a time, mixing thoroughly between each addition.

3. Pour batter into prepared dish and bake 30 minutes until a toothpick inserted in center comes out clean. Serve warm or at room temperature.

· · · · · · · · · · · · · ·

PENELOPE

In the show, there were lots of clues as to Penelope's alter ego: Her first scene presented her with a large quill in her hair, her nickname is Pen, and she had a compelling reason to uncover Marina Thompson's pregnancy to sink her prospects of marrying her beloved Colin Bridgerton.

Eloise's Strawberry Tart

A truly independent young woman if there ever was one, Eloise, not at all inclined to enter the marriage market, prefers to observe the affairs of the ton from the safe distance of her notebook. Yet she is not immune to temptation, including any that might emanate from the Bridgerton kitchen. She loves this strawberry tart so much it is named after her.

MAKES 1 (9") PIE

For Crust
1⅔ cups all-purpose flour
¼ cup granulated sugar
½ teaspoon salt
½ cup plus 2 tablespoons unsalted butter
2 large egg yolks
⅛ teaspoon vanilla extract
1 tablespoon cold water

For Almond Paste
¾ cup almonds
2 tablespoons agave nectar or light corn syrup
2 tablespoons Madeira or port
½ cup confectioners' sugar
2 tablespoons unsalted butter

For Strawberry Glaze
⅓ cup strawberry jam
¼ cup sirop de cassis
1½ cups whole strawberries, hulled and sliced

CONTINUED

1. To make Crust: Preheat oven to 350°F.

2. In a food processor, briefly blend all ingredients. Remove from processor and knead dough lightly (up to 2 minutes maximum) and press into a greased 9" springform tart pan.

3. Carefully press a sheet of foil into Crust, using your fingers to fit it into all corners. Place pastry weights or baking beans in foil and bake 45–60 minutes, depending on Crust thickness.

4. To make Almond Paste: Roast almonds in a medium skillet over low heat 10 minutes, then grind in a processor with agave nectar or corn syrup, Madeira or port, confectioners' sugar, and butter. Set aside.

5. To make Strawberry Glaze: Warm jam in a small pot over low heat 4 minutes. Add sirop de cassis.

6. To assemble: Spread Almond Paste in baked Crust. Place sliced strawberries snugly in Crust and cover with Strawberry Glaze.

7. Refrigerate tart 1 hour until set. Bring to room temperature 1 hour before serving.

. . . .

STRAWBERRIES

English strawberries were a big deal in the early 1800s.
English gardeners were known for growing the largest strawberries,
a monumental achievement given that strawberries in Europe
were tiny, like the wild varieties we see today.

Hyacinth's Royal Rubies
Chocolate Bark

Though it was not customary for the governess to teach the children cooking, or any other physical labor for that matter, it surely has been done. This is a fun and easy way to make a colorful dessert with children. The recipe below works just as well with milk, dark, or white chocolate. Wrap your bark prettily with a bow to make an impressive gift. While our beloved Bridgertons didn't actually have access to berry-pink ruby chocolate, they surely enjoyed their jewels.

SERVES 6

1 cup ruby chocolate chips
¼ cup freeze-dried blueberries, raspberries, and/or strawberries
¼ cup dry-roasted slivered almonds or chopped shelled dry-roasted pistachios
1 teaspoon Himalayan sea salt (optional)

1. Line a baking sheet with wax paper.

2. Place chocolate chips in a small microwave-safe bowl and microwave on medium in 30-second intervals, stirring well between cook times until chips are melting but retain shape.

3. Using a spatula, spread chocolate onto wax paper. While chocolate is still warm and pliable, sprinkle on remaining ingredients, and then refrigerate baking sheet 30 minutes or until firm. Once firm, break or slice into shards.

GOVERNESSES

A governess was a live-in teacher for the children of the upper class. She would have to be well educated and from a middle-class family. Generally, it was not considered an envious vocation. Governesses would be forced to work long hours for low pay and would often be lonely and isolated, as they were of higher status than the servants but lower than the family members who employed them.

Dark Walk Lava Cakes

No respectable lady should ever be seen upon the Dark Walk, especially with two men! For whatever cannot be seen in the darkness can only become speculation, which, given the right nudging, can easily become scandal. These Dark Walk Lava Cakes are best eaten immediately, while the center is hot and succulent, and before the chilled gaze of Cressida chances upon them.

MAKES 6 CAKES

1 (10-ounce) bag chocolate chips
¾ cup unsalted butter
4 large eggs
2 tablespoons granulated sugar
2 teaspoons espresso powder or instant coffee
½ cup confectioners' sugar

1. Preheat oven to 350°F and grease six ramekins with nonstick cooking spray.

2. In a large microwave-safe bowl, heat chocolate chips and butter on high in 30-second intervals, stirring between each cook time until chips are melted.

3. In a large bowl, use a hand mixer to beat eggs, granulated sugar, and coffee together approximately 6 minutes or until frothy. Gently fold into melted chocolate mixture and split among prepared ramekins.

4. Bake 17 minutes or until sides are firm but tops are still a little jiggly. Sift confectioners' sugar over cakes and serve immediately.

. . . .

THE DARK WALK

During the Regency, the Dark Walk was central to nighttime amusement.
A "pleasure garden," this is where people would gather and listen to music, dance, and drink.
It could also be a very dangerous place for women, for if one were to lose her virtue,
whether by choice or not, she would likely have to marry the man involved.

Gunter's Ice Cream

*Simon's been known to do some seriously lascivious licking, and while out
in public no less. It could have been due to the chemical reactions taking place in
the Gunter's Tea Shop between him and Daphne, but I suspect it had more
to do with the glorious richness of this classic Regency ice cream.*

MAKES 4 CUPS

¾ cup unsalted butter
1 cup salted cashews
½ teaspoon sea salt
2 cups whipping cream
1 cup half-and-half
1 cup granulated sugar
1 teaspoon vanilla extract

1. In a medium saucepan over low heat, melt butter.

2. Using a coffee grinder or mortar and pestle, grind cashews to a powder. Add to pan along with salt and cook slowly until butter browns, stirring constantly. Remove from heat and set aside to cool.

3. In a medium pot over medium heat, cook cream, half-and-half, sugar, and vanilla and mix until sugar has dissolved, about 10 minutes.

4. Pour cream mixture into an ice cream maker and run according to manufacturer's instructions until mixture gets very thick.

5. Add cashew butter into ice cream maker and continue to run 30 seconds to integrate. Serve, or freeze in a large sealed container up to 3 weeks.

SUGAR

During the 1800s, sugar was sold in the form of a cone wrapped in paper and sealed with a wax stamp. These cones could weigh a few pounds each. Households would have a tool called a *nipper* to remove sugar from the cone.

Revolutionary Parmesan Ice Cream

*To our dear, faithful reader: It cannot be overstated that our beloved
Bridgertons cannot get enough of creams and cheeses! To enjoy these savory
flavors while also staying afloat of high society, mix these two treasures
with ice for a respite from a warm evening.*

MAKES 4 CUPS

2 cups heavy whipping cream, divided
¹⁄₃ cup grated Parmesan cheese
¹⁄₂ teaspoon ground white pepper
1 cup half-and-half
1 teaspoon vanilla extract
2 tablespoons aged balsamic vinegar (optional)

1. In a medium pot over medium heat, add 1 cup cream, cheese, and white
   pepper and whisk constantly until cheese is melted, about 5 minutes.

2. Slowly add remaining 1 cup cream, half-and-half, and vanilla while
   continuing to whisk.

3. Pour into a large bowl to cool about 30 minutes. Place in refrigerator 1 hour.
   Then pour into an ice cream maker and follow manufacturer's instructions
   to mix until creamy. Serve, or freeze in a large sealed container up to
   2 weeks. Garnish ice cream with balsamic vinegar before serving if desired.

COLD HOUSES

During the Regency, those of high social standing who had large estates
would surely have their own cold houses. These structures were packed with large
blocks of ice that were either cut from local rivers and ponds in the winter or brought in
by ships from glaciers in the north. They were well insulated to keep from
thawing, much like Lady Cowper.

The Waltz

*Just as Daphne and Simon charmed the ball with their waltz, this dance
of fruit and rum will be hard to take your eyes off of. The cocktail is breathtaking
based on its ruby color alone, but the taste is the true nonpareil of the evening.*

SERVES 1

For Strawberry Pomegranate Syrup
½ cup (approximately 10) sliced and hulled fresh strawberries
1 cup pomegranate juice
1 cup granulated sugar

For Cocktail
2 ounces dark rum
¾ ounce Strawberry Pomegranate Syrup (see recipe)
¾ ounce lime juice

1. To make Strawberry Pomegranate Syrup: Blend strawberries in a blender
   with pomegranate juice and strain into a small saucepan. Add sugar, and
   heat over low heat until sugar is dissolved. Store refrigerated up to 1 week.

2. To make Cocktail: Combine all ingredients in a cocktail shaker filled with ice
   and shake vigorously. Strain into a coupe or martini glass.

THE WALTZ

The waltz started to become popular in the early 1800s in London
and was initially viewed as immoral and dangerous since it required considerable
contact between the two dancers.

Duchess Champagne Cocktail

At the evening's ball, the excitement is tangible. Matchmakers from
all sides of Grosvenor Square are vying to secure the season's worthiest suitors.
The proper drink can seduce the intended while offering cool refreshment from
the heat of courting. This cocktail combines elegant sparkling wine with
fresh pineapple juice to make a stylish drink for your guests.

SERVES 1

¼ cup lemon sorbet
4 ounces dry sparkling white wine
2 ounces pineapple juice
2 dashes aromatic Angostura bitters
1 teaspoon granulated sugar
1 slice pineapple

1. Add sorbet to a coupe or martini glass and freeze 20 minutes before serving.
2. Add wine, pineapple juice, bitters, and sugar to a cocktail shaker and fill with ice. Shake vigorously and strain into glass over sorbet. Garnish with pineapple slice.

CHAMPAGNE

In the 900s, the region of Champagne became known for producing red wine. This area has cold winter temperatures, producing light, acidic grapes. These temperatures also lead to a slowing of the fermentation process for many months of the year, which, during the early years of production, often caused bottles to explode during warmer months when fermentation sped up, causing bubbles. Bottles that survived the CO_2 buildup were bubbly, which, even during the time of monk Dom Pérignon (mid to late 1600s), was considered a failure.

Whistledown Gimlet

It is rumored that the gimlet is Lady Whistledown's drink of choice. Should you ever meet her, serve her this to stay on her good side. It also works on mothers-in-law. This recipe is based on the classic British cocktail, the gimlet, but is elaborated with exotic, imported spices—just what Lady Whistledown would have been sipping at happy hour…or teatime.

SERVES 1

For Rose and Earl Grey Teatime Cordial (makes 16 ounces)
1 bag rose tea
1 bag Earl Grey tea
8 ounces water
Zest and juice from 8 small limes, divided
8 ounces granulated sugar
$1/2$ ounce white vinegar

For Gimlet
2 ounces Plymouth Gin Navy Strength
2 dashes Scrappy's Cardamom Bitters
$1/2$ ounce Rose and Earl Grey Teatime Cordial (see recipe)
$1/4$ ounce elderflower liqueur
1 lime peel
1 dried rosebud

1. To make Rose and Earl Grey Teatime Cordial: In a small saucepan over low heat, combine tea bags, water, lime zest, sugar, and vinegar. Simmer 10 minutes or until sugar dissolves. Remove from heat and cool about 30 minutes.

2. When cool, strain into a small container. Stir in lime juice (approximately 8 ounces). Refrigerate up to 2 weeks.

CONTINUED

3. To make Gimlet: Add gin, bitters, Rose and Earl Grey Teatime Cordial, and liqueur to a cocktail shaker filled with ice and shake vigorously. Strain into a teacup or rocks glass over a few ice cubes or pieces of rounded ice. Garnish with lime peel and rosebud.

. . . . .

GIN

Plymouth Gin is the oldest working gin distillery in England, using the same recipe since 1793. Their motto is: "Plymouth Gin Navy Strength Intense, bold and aromatic. For almost two centuries, no Royal Navy ship left port without it." Gin, flavored with juniper berries, was developed for its medicinal properties, but the taste the British developed for it proved to require its own medicine!

Granville Mule

When Benedict accepted Sir Granville's invitation to a wild party at his art studio, he was not sure what to expect. The fabulous art world was bursting with impropriety! As soon as Benedict met Madame Delacroix, passions quickly heated up. This colorful cocktail is just the thing to kick off an evening of debauchery.

SERVES 1

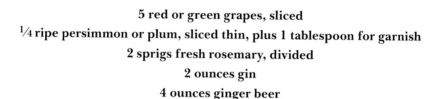

5 red or green grapes, sliced
¼ ripe persimmon or plum, sliced thin, plus 1 tablespoon for garnish
2 sprigs fresh rosemary, divided
2 ounces gin
4 ounces ginger beer

1. Add grapes, persimmon or plum, 1 sprig rosemary, and gin to a cocktail shaker and muddle to express juices from fruit. Fill shaker with ice and shake 10 seconds.

2. Strain into a julep cup over crushed ice. Top with ginger beer. Garnish with remaining tablespoon persimmon or plum and remaining sprig rosemary.

EXTRAMARITAL AFFAIRS

The Regency was a time of glorious excess, and members of the upper echelons of society applied this mindset to sex. And, because betrothals were often about social standing rather than love, many an engaged or married man or woman would find themselves in an extramarital affair. Heaven help the upper-class individual who, like Anthony, fell in love with someone outside their social circle!

Debutante Punch

This is a must-have when hosting a ball or other formal gathering, as it is a quick and quite attractive way to enchant even the most bored of debutantes. Leave a space open on your dance ticket for later on in the evening when things really heat up and the heart begins to wander.

SERVES 10

1 cup mixed fresh berries

5 slices orange, divided

5 slices lemon, divided

3 sprigs fresh rosemary

1 star anise seed

3 cinnamon sticks

3 whole cloves

1 (750-ml) bottle merlot

6 ounces brandy

4 ounces pulp-free orange juice

6 dashes orange bitters

2 ounces fresh lemon juice

1. Fill a large plastic or silicone sealable container ¾ of the way full with water. Add mixed berries, 3 slices orange, 3 slices lemon, and rosemary, cover, and freeze overnight.

2. In a large saucepan over medium heat, dry-toast spices 1 minute or until fragrant. Reduce heat to low and add merlot, brandy, and orange juice. Cook 10 minutes. Do not let boil.

3. Strain wine mixture into a large sealable container. Add bitters. Refrigerate about 3 hours until cool or before serving. Serve in a large punch bowl with frozen mixed berry mixture and remaining citrus slices.

. . . .

PUNCH

Punch was an extremely popular drink of the Regency era, especially among men of society who needed their own version of teatime. Original recipes included brandy and rum and were loaded with spices, making it quite the delicious drink.

Heartbreak Cure

While the pursuit of true love can carry with it lofty joy, for our love-lusting ton, it also comes with heartbreak. When desolate in love and romance, one seeks the warmth of good company and, perhaps, a soothing drink. This passion fruit cocktail will energize the spirit and mend the heart.

SERVES 1

For Passion Fruit Liqueur
1 (750-ml) bottle vodka
2 medium passion fruits, peeled, blended, and strained
2 tablespoons granulated sugar

For Cocktail
2 ounces gin
1 ounce vodka
$\frac{1}{2}$ ounce Passion Fruit Liqueur (see recipe)
1 fresh blackberry
1 small lemon peel

1. To make Passion Fruit Liqueur: Add all ingredients to a large, sealable container and mix. Let sugar dissolve 48 hours at room temperature.
2. To make Cocktail: Add all ingredients to a mixing glass. Fill with ice and mix using a bar spoon 20 seconds or until cocktail is very chilled.
3. Strain into a martini glass. Garnish with blackberry and lemon peel.

COCKTAILS

From 1803 to about 1862, cocktails were in the realm of gamblers, hustlers, and so-called "loose women." Drinking a cocktail made you a little bit edgy and perhaps all the more alluring. Although most polite society would turn up their nose at cocktails, these drinks were quickly becoming more and more popular by the minute. During after-hours activities, one could expect to find the most unusual and full-strength cocktails.

The Gentlemen's Club Boilermaker

While the esteemed guests are hard at work gambling away their fortunes over whiskey and rum, Anthony and Simon are quite content on resolving the matter of Daphne's marriage to Simon. It would appear that the one thing capable of ruining a friendship is the love of a woman. Lift a card from each glass and take a shot as your friends time you.

SERVES 1

For Tart Lemonade
4 ounces fresh lemon juice
1 ounce simple syrup (equal parts water and granulated sugar blended until dissolved)
3 ounces water

For Cocktail
1 ounce dark rum
1 ounce Tart Lemonade (see recipe)
1 ounce crème de cassis

1. To make Tart Lemonade: Mix ingredients together in a small bowl or pitcher.
2. To make Cocktail: Pour rum into a shot glass. Pour Tart Lemonade in a second shot glass. Pour crème de cassis into a third shot glass. Place a playing card on top of each glass and serve.

. . . .

GENTLEMEN'S CLUB

A membership at a high-class gentlemen's club was compulsory for any respectable ton. These were very exclusive, and new members had to be voted in by the use of colored balls. Each member would secretly place a white ball for "yes" or a black ball for "no" in a box. This is the origin of "being blackballed."

US/Metric Conversion Charts

Volume Conversions

US Volume Measure	Metric Equivalent
⅛ teaspoon	0.5 milliliter
¼ teaspoon	1 milliliter
½ teaspoon	2 milliliters
1 teaspoon	5 milliliters
½ tablespoon	7 milliliters
1 tablespoon (3 teaspoons)	15 milliliters
2 tablespoons (1 fluid ounce)	30 milliliters
¼ cup (4 tablespoons)	60 milliliters
⅓ cup	90 milliliters
½ cup (4 fluid ounces)	125 milliliters
⅔ cup	160 milliliters
¾ cup (6 fluid ounces)	180 milliliters
1 cup (16 tablespoons)	250 milliliters
1 pint (2 cups)	500 milliliters
1 quart (4 cups)	1 liter (about)

Weight Conversions

US Weight Measure	Metric Equivalent
½ ounce	15 grams
1 ounce	30 grams
2 ounces	60 grams
3 ounces	85 grams
¼ pound (4 ounces)	115 grams
½ pound (8 ounces)	225 grams
¾ pound (12 ounces)	340 grams
1 pound (16 ounces)	454 grams

US/Metric Conversion Charts

Baking Pan Sizes

American	Metric
8 × 1½ inch round baking pan	20 × 4 cm cake tin
9 × 1½ inch round baking pan	23 × 3.5 cm cake tin
11 × 7 × 1½ inch baking pan	28 × 18 × 4 cm baking tin
13 × 9 × 2 inch baking pan	30 × 20 × 5 cm baking tin
2 quart rectangular baking dish	30 × 20 × 3 cm baking tin
15 × 10 × 2 inch baking pan	30 × 25 × 2 cm baking tin (Swiss roll tin)
9 inch pie plate	22 × 4 or 23 × 4 cm pie plate
7 or 8 inch springform pan	18 or 20 cm springform or loose bottom cake tin
9 × 5 × 3 inch loaf pan	23 × 13 × 7 cm or 2 lb narrow loaf or pate tin
1½ quart casserole	1.5 liter casserole
2 quart casserole	2 liter casserole

Oven Temperature Conversions

Degrees Fahrenheit	Degrees Celsius
200 degrees F	95 degrees C
250 degrees F	120 degrees C
275 degrees F	135 degrees C
300 degrees F	150 degrees C
325 degrees F	160 degrees C
350 degrees F	180 degrees C
375 degrees F	190 degrees C
400 degrees F	205 degrees C
425 degrees F	220 degrees C
450 degrees F	230 degrees C

Index

B

Bacon bites, 181
Baked salmon, Brimsley's, 160–61
Balls, Regency life and, 68
Banana, Cavendish, 37
Banana, in Prudence's Breakfast Pudding, 37
Barley, about, 122
Barley, heritage mushroom cream of, 122
Bartlett, Sabrina, 141
Basil
    Basil Garlic Sauce, 160
    Pesto, 156–57
Beau monde, about, 20
The Beau Monde Biscuits, 20–21
Beef
    about: meat pies and pâtés, 59; nose-to-tail butchery, 167
    Clyvedon Market Pies, 182–83
    Oxford Roasted Beef Heart with Lemon Confit, 167
    Regency Pie, 164–66
    Royal Indulgence Biscuits with Gravy, 29
Beets
    about: associations of, 142; uses during the Regency, 142
    The Footman's Finest Roasted Vegetables, 132–34
    Seductively Red Beet Salad with Fennel, Yogurt, and Granola, 142–43
Bejeweled Oatmeal, 24–25
Benedict's Mushroom Miniatures, 64–65
Benedict's Perfected Cod à la Hollandaise, 149
Berries
    about: barberries, 36; gooseberries, 77, 188; strawberries in the early 1800s, 206

    Chocolate-Dipped Duke and Duchess Strawberries, 83
    Debutante Punch, 218–19
    Eloise's Strawberry Tart, 205–6
    Fruit Compote, 24–25
    High Society Scones, 35–36
    Household Hasty-Bake Oatmeal Pies with Sugared Berries, 27–28
    Hyacinth's Royal Rubies Chocolate Bark, 207
    Lady Featherington's Society Sponge Cake, 80–82
    Macerated Berries, 80
    Marina's Letter Cookies, 90–91
    The Royal Flummery, 193
    Rumor-Stirring Blueberry Lavender Fizz, 102–3
    Teatime Gooseberry Pie Lemonade, 77
Bet-Winning Butternut Squash Soup, 111–12
Biscuits (bread)
    about: buttermilk and, 29
    The Beau Monde Biscuits, 20–21
    Royal Indulgence Biscuits with Gravy, 29
Biscuits (cookies). *See* Cookies
Boilermaker, 221
Boxer's Best Sausage Doughnuts, 32–33
Brandy, in Debutante Punch, 218–19
Breads and such. *See also* Sandwiches/miniatures
    about: mini muffins, 94
    The Beau Monde Biscuits, 20–21
    Colin's Favorite Corn Cakes, 129
    First Bloom Mini Muffins with Blue Buttercream Frosting, 92–94
    Francesca's Fried Dough, 22
    High Society Scones, 35–36
    Marry for Love Mini Muffins with Cinnamon Streusel, 96–97

About the Author

Lex Taylor is the author of *Grill Fire*; was the winner of Esquire Network's *The Next Great Burger*; and has been featured on *Chopped* and *Beat Bobby Flay*. Lex specializes in traditional cooking techniques such as smoking, curing, pickling, and making pastries. Combining his love of food, history, and popular culture, Lex is known to improvise amazing recipes for popular series, including his favorite, *Bridgerton*. You can follow Lex on *Instagram* at @the.north.feast.